M000035836

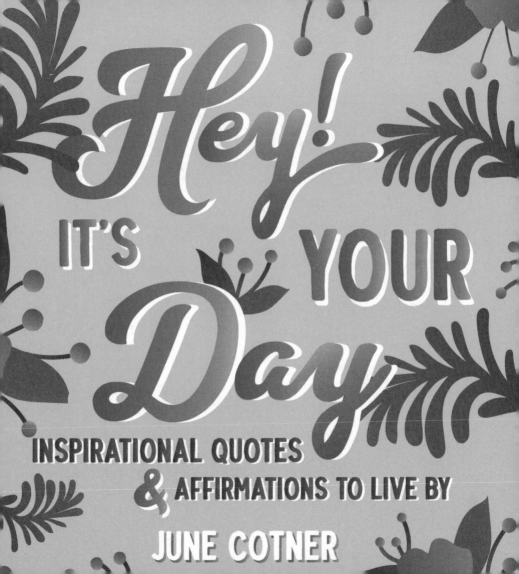

Hey! It's YOUR Day

INSPIRATIONAL QUOTES & AFFIRMATIONS TO LIVE BY

JUNE COTNER

Also by June Cotner

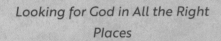
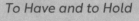

Hey! IT'S YOUR Day

INSPIRATIONAL QUOTES & AFFIRMATIONS TO LIVE BY

JUNE COTNER

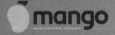

mango

CORAL GABLES

For permission requests, please contact the publisher at:

Mango Publishing Group
2850 Douglas Road, 2nd Floor
Coral Gables, FL 33134 USA
info@mango.bz

For special orders, quantity sales, course adoptions and corporate sales, please email the publisher at sales@mango.bz. For trade and wholesale sales, please contact Ingram Publisher Services at customer.service@ingramcontent.com or +1.800.509.4887.

Hey! It's Your Day: Inspirational Quotes & Affirmations to Live By

ISBN: (p) 978-1-64250-393-7 (e) 978-1-64250-394-4

BISAC: REF019000—REFERENCE / Quotations

LCCN: 2020946324

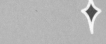

FOR JIM, ALWAYS

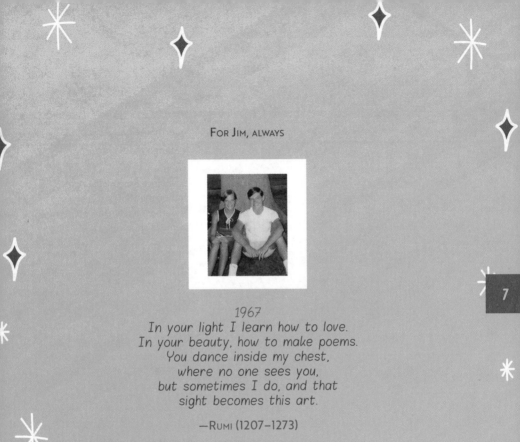

1967
In your light I learn how to love.
In your beauty, how to make poems.
You dance inside my chest,
where no one sees you,
but sometimes I do, and that
sight becomes this art.

—RUMI (1207–1273)

TRANSLATED BY COLEMAN BARKS

Table of Contents

A Letter to Readers

I've been a quote collector since I was fourteen. In fact, I still have the same notebook, started in my teen years, that I used to record words that moved me. At an early age, I sought out quotes about "making the most of your day." I also liked short quotes that became affirmations for living. These affirmations have remained a powerful force in my life, and you'll find many of them throughout this book.

Sadly, I also gravitated to quotes on grieving because my dear mother died when I was eleven and my maternal grandfather died when I was seventeen. I no longer had these two incredible people acting as guides in my life, so I turned to others' words to help me along. Hundreds of times, if not thousands, I found solace from four lines in Wordsworth's "Ode on Intimations of Immortality from Recollections of Early Childhood":

> Though nothing can bring back the hour
> Of splendour in the grass, of glory in the flower;
> We will grieve not, rather find
> Strength in what remains behind...

—WILLIAM WORDSWORTH

I continued collecting and curating quotes as I entered adulthood. During my college years, I loved finding quotes about both appreciating life and achievement. The following quote by Carlos Castaneda became popular when I was in college. It came from his 1968 book, *The Teachings of Don Juan: A Yaqui Way of Knowledge.*

> For me there is only the traveling on paths that have heart, on any path that may have heart, and the only worthwhile challenge is to traverse its full length—and there I travel looking, looking breathlessly.

—CARLOS CASTANEDA

At the start of my full-time work life when I was twenty-two, I was drawn to quotes about passion and success, and general

quotes about life. Here is one I wrote out, pasted a pretty picture above, and put on my office wall.

> *No longer forward or behind*
> *I look in hope or fear;*
> *But, grateful, take the good I find,*
> *The best of now and here.*

—John Greenleaf Whittier

When I became a mother, my priorities changed so much that finding inspirational quotes about children, parenthood, family, and motherhood helped me navigate this new path. When my kids were still under the age of five, I stood in front of my refrigerator countless times to read this magnet:

> *Cleaning your house while your kids are still growing*
> *is like shoveling the walk before it stops snowing.*

—Phyllis Diller

If inspiration didn't help me then as a young mother, at least I was comforted with humor. While humor can be a powerful healer, we often need more than just amusement along our journey in life. I went through a divorce mid-life and found I needed quotes on challenges, comfort, courage, faith, forgiveness, grieving (again), hope, perspective, reflections, renewal, and wisdom. It has been a labor of love as I've collected quotes that reflect upon all of these topics, which you'll find in *Hey! It's Your Day*. Here's one from the "Comfort" section:

> *The human spirit is stronger than anything*
> *that can happen to it.*
>
> —C. C. Scott

Now, I've been happily married for over twenty-five years to my high school sweetheart, and I'm the mother of two grown children and the grandmother of four. The topics of aging, children, family, gratitude, inspiration, kindness, perspective, reflections, simplicity, and simple reminders have become especially meaningful to me. I want to make the most of every day, and two "author unknown" quotes offer the daily perspective I seek:

*What a wonderful thought it is
that some of the best days of our lives
haven't happened yet.*

And...

*Do not regret growing older.
It's a privilege denied to many.*

When I was close to completing this book, I realized I had
forgotten to include a section about pets! If it had not been for
my dogs and cats through the years, I don't know how I would
have gotten through many challenges and long periods of grief.
So, in honor of our dear pets:

*Sometimes you don't need words to feel better:
you just need the nearness of your dog.*

—Natalie Lloyd

Dear reader, I don't know where you are in your life's journey, but I'm pretty sure you will find many quotes in *Hey! It's Your Day* that will inspire you every day. You have a whole book ahead of you, so I'll close with a short, affirming quote, which has guided me for many years:

Nothing is worth more than this day.

—JOHANN WOLFGANG VON GOETHE

15

June Cotner

www.junecotner.com | june@junecotner.com

Facebook: @June.Cotner.Books (author page)
LinkedIn: www.linkedin.com/in/junecotner
Instagram: @JuneCotner
Twitter: @JuneCotner

Adventure

When I was young, adventure meant going off with my sister or a group of friends to explore—whether that meant going to a mall and observing shoppers, biking to a faraway lake, or playing games in the woods behind our house. Today, not only does adventure mean being inspired by new experiences when I travel, but also being inspired by seeing everyday experiences with fresh eyes. It could be paying close attention to what I see on walks and hikes or even the thrilling experience of discovering something I love via online research.

The joy of life comes from our encounters with new experiences.

—JON KRAKAUER

Each day is an adventure in discovering the meaning of life.

—JACK CANFIELD

It is good to have an end to journey toward;
but it is the journey that matters, in the end.

—URSULA K. LE GUIN

18

To awaken quite alone in a strange town is one of the most
pleasant sensations in the world.
You are surrounded by adventure.

—FREYA STARK

My favorite thing is to go where I've never been.

—DIANE ARBUS

The voyage of discovery is not in seeking new landscapes,
but in having new eyes.

—MARCEL PROUST

Stuff your eyes with wonder, live as if you'd drop dead in ten seconds. See the world. It's more fantastic than any dream made or paid for in factories.

—RAY BRADBURY

A mind that is stretched by a new experience can never go back to its old dimensions.

—OLIVER WENDELL HOLMES

There is no greater joy than to have an endlessly changing horizon, for each day to have a new and different sun.

—CHRIS MCCANDLESS

The most fulfilling adventures happen when you start your journey without knowing where you're going, because only then are you free to experience the unexpected detours you're meant to take.

—A. J. DARKHOLME

Life is either a great adventure or nothing.

—HELEN KELLER

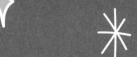

May your trails be crooked, winding, lonesome, dangerous,
leading to the most amazing view.

—EDWARD ABBEY

Life is adventure, not predicament.

—JAMES BROUGHTON

Twenty years from now you will be more disappointed by the
things you didn't do than by the ones you did do. So throw off
the bowlines. Sail away from the safe harbor. Catch the trade
winds in your sails. Explore. Dream. Discover.

—H. JACKSON BROWN JR.

Each thing she learned became a part of herself
to be used over and over in new adventures.

—KATE SEREDY

Serendipity. Look for something, find something else, and
realize that what you've found is more suited to your needs
than what you thought you were looking for.

—LAWRENCE BLOCK

Adventure isn't hanging on a rope off the side of a mountain. Adventure is an attitude that we must apply to the day to day obstacles of life—facing new challenges, seizing new opportunities, testing our resources against the unknown and in the process, discovering our own unique potential.

—JOHN AMATT

Adventure is worthwhile in itself.

—AMELIA EARHART

21

I think over again my small adventures, my fears, These small ones that seemed so big. For all those vital things I had to get and to reach. And yet there is only one great thing, The only thing. To live and see the great day that dawns And the light that fills the world.

—INUIT SONG

Aging

My take on aging is that we start aging from the day we are born, but we really don't feel like we're "aging" until our thirties, when our bodies grumble just a bit with minor aches and pains. At this point, many of us think: *Well, what do I want to do with the rest of my life?* The quotes in this chapter will give you many ideas and perspectives for living each day of your life with zest and enthusiasm. To age well is to grow in wisdom and experience. I've learned over the course of my years to appreciate things that, when I was younger, I would never have considered a blessing. I hope these quotes inspire you to think about the blessings of passing years in your own life.

You are never too old to set another goal
or dream a new dream.

—C. S. Lewis

When I'm old I'm never going to say, "I didn't do this" or "I
regret that." I'm going to say, "I don't regret a damn thing.
I came, I went, and I did it all."

—Kim Basinger

As I get older, I realize that the thing
I value the most is good-heartedness.

—Alice Walker

What a wonderful life I've had! I only wish I'd realized it sooner.

—Colette

In cemeteries, the same thought always arises for me:
"They come and they go. We come and we go."
This thought gives me a sense of peace.

—Mary Pipher

Anyone who stops learning is old, whether at twenty or eighty.
Anyone who keeps learning stays young.
The greatest thing in life is to keep your mind young.

—HENRY FORD

What becomes fragile when we age is not our bodies
as much as our egos.
The best time to take some daring steps is when we get older.

—HELEN HAYES

We turn not older in years,
but newer every day.

—EMILY DICKINSON

The longer I live
the more beautiful life becomes.

—FRANK LLOYD WRIGHT

What a wonderful thought it is
that some of the best days of our lives
haven't happened yet.

—ANNE FRANK

Do not regret growing older.
It's a privilege denied to many.

—AUTHOR UNKNOWN

You don't get to choose how you're going to die.
Or when. But you can decide how you're going to live now.

—JOAN BAEZ

Life should not be a journey to the grave with the intention of
arriving safely in a pretty and well preserved body, but rather
to skid in broadside in a cloud of smoke, thoroughly used up,
totally worn out, and loudly proclaiming "Wow! What a Ride!"

—HUNTER S. THOMPSON

Attitude

Attitude is a quality we develop and hopefully improve upon as we age. It's that rock-solid tenacity that will keep you committed to your goals and your perspective on life. Ideally, it should be so grounded that it's your automatic "go-to" thought or action. But developing a great attitude about life takes time. The quotes in this chapter will give you many ideas for affirmations on living life with an upbeat attitude. How we choose to respond to events can be one of the most important things we can learn to control. While life will frequently throw us curveballs, it is our attitude that can make a profound difference in a positive outcome.

*The only difference between a good day
and a bad day is your attitude*

—DENNIS S. BROWN

*Expect the most wonderful things to happen,
not in the future but right now.*

—EILEEN CADDY

*It's not what happens to you,
but how you react to it that matters.*

—EPICTETUS

28

*There are only two ways to live your life.
One is as though nothing is a miracle.
The other is as though everything is a miracle.*

—ALBERT EINSTEIN

I never lose sight of the fact that just being is fun.

—KATHARINE HEPBURN

*The more you praise and celebrate your life,
the more there is in life to celebrate.*

—OPRAH WINFREY

Do not let what you cannot do interfere with what you can do.

—JOHN WOODEN

The greatest revolution in our generation is that of human
beings, who by changing the inner attitudes of their minds
can change the outer aspects of their lives.

—WILLIAM JAMES

If you concentrate on finding whatever is good in every
situation, you will discover that your life will suddenly be filled
with gratitude, a feeling that nurtures the soul.

—HAROLD KUSHNER

If you look at what you have in life, you'll always have more. If
you look at what you don't have in life, you'll never have enough.

—OPRAH WINFREY

It's never about how little we have.
It is about what our little has the potential to become.

—CHRISTINE CAINE

Nothing is worth more than this day.
You cannot relive yesterday.
Tomorrow is still beyond your reach.

—JOHANN WOLFGANG VON GOETHE

Concern yourself not with what you tried and failed in,
but with what is still possible to do.

—POPE JOHN XXIII

The universe is change; our life is what our thoughts make it.

—MARCUS AURELIUS

Your living is determined not so much by what life
brings to you as the attitude you bring to life.

—KAHLIL GIBRAN

Many girls grew up dreaming of a hero to save them.
I grew up dreaming of becoming one.

—LESLEY, AGE EIGHTEEN, FROM *STRONG IS THE NEW PRETTY*

We either make ourselves miserable,
or we make ourselves strong.
The amount of work is the same.

—CARLOS CASTANEDA

30

Belief

Belief is kind of a tricky thing. How do we figure out what is true or false—and determine what we want to believe in? One of the best ways is to be inspired by positive, uplifting quotes from people of integrity, which you'll find in this chapter. Belief is an attitude of how we see the world. Believing in ourselves can also be a profound touchstone as we navigate life.

32

To bring anything into your life, imagine that it's already there.

—RICHARD BACH

Whoever believes in the good in people,
draws forth the good in people.

—JEAN PAUL

33

In spite of everything,
I still believe people are really good at heart.

—ANNE FRANK

Even if I knew that tomorrow the world would go to pieces, I
would still plant my apple tree.

—MARTIN LUTHER

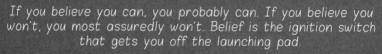

If you believe you can, you probably can. If you believe you won't, you most assuredly won't. Belief is the ignition switch that gets you off the launching pad.

—Denis Waitley

For me there is only the traveling on paths that have heart, on any path that may have heart, and the only worthwhile challenge is to traverse its full length—and there I travel looking, looking breathlessly.

—Carlos Castaneda

34

I do not believe today everything I believed yesterday; I wonder will I believe tomorrow everything I believe today.

—Matthew Arnold

Whether you think you can or can't—you are right.

—Henry Ford

Challenges

We encounter challenges every day—whether it's working hard to come up with a solution to a difficult problem or dealing with the day-to-day challenges of creating a harmonious life. Often, it's so easy to become just plain stuck. When you need a pick-me-up or insight regarding a setback in your life, the quotes in this chapter offer a great starting point. You'll see ideas you can apply to your own problems and develop a better perspective in dealing with them. And with every new challenge resolved, a new strength emerges.

There is no such thing as a problem without a gift for you in its
hands. You seek problems because you need their gifts.

—RICHARD BACH

Whatever brings you down, will eventually make you stronger.

—ALEX MORGAN

Don't despair!... Let the waters run...
that which is for you will never get lost or die.

—SPANISH SAYING

36

The sun is a daily reminder
that we too can rise again from the darkness,
that we too can shine our own light.

—S. AJNA

I have sometimes been wildly, despairingly, acutely miserable,
racked with sorrow; but through it all I still know quite certainly
that just to be alive is a grand thing.

—AGATHA CHRISTIE

Each time we face our fear,
we gain strength, courage, and confidence in the doing.

—THEODORE ROOSEVELT

Challenges are gifts that force us to search for a new center of gravity. Don't fight them. Just find a different way to stand.

—OPRAH WINFREY

Difficult times have helped me to understand better than before how infinitely rich and beautiful life is in every way and that so many things that one goes worrying about are of no importance whatsoever.

—ISAK DINESEN

In the middle of difficulty lies opportunity.

—ALBERT EINSTEIN

Hanging onto resentment is letting someone you despise live rent-free in your head.

—ANN LANDERS

We must not wish for the disappearance of our troubles but for the grace to transform them.

—SIMONE WEIL

Some days there won't be a song in your heart. Sing anyway.

—EMORY AUSTIN

There is a crack in everything That's how the light gets in.

—LEONARD COHEN

Don't let a bad day make you feel like you have a bad life.

—AUTHOR UNKNOWN

Do not pray for tasks equal to your powers. Pray for powers
equal to your tasks. Then the doing of your work shall be no
miracle, but you shall be the miracle.

—PHILLIPS BROOKS

The period of greatest gain in knowledge and experience is the
most difficult period in one's life. Through a difficult period, you
can learn; you can develop inner strength, determination, and
courage to face the problems.

—H. H. DALAI LAMA

Ask yourself this question: "Will this matter a year from now?"

—RICHARD CARLSON

Ironically, gratitude's most powerful mysteries are often
revealed when we are struggling
in the midst of personal turmoil.

—SARAH BAN BREATHNACH

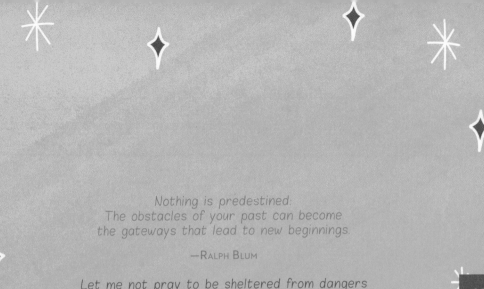

Nothing is predestined:
The obstacles of your past can become
the gateways that lead to new beginnings.

—RALPH BLUM

Let me not pray to be sheltered from dangers
but to be fearless when facing them.

—RABINDRANATH TAGORE

Not all storms come to disrupt your path.
Some come to clear your path.

—AUTHOR UNKNOWN

39

Change

Change is often unexpected, yet it is ongoing throughout life. It is interconnected with challenges, faith, and hope. You're probably currently living with new changes in your life, whether it's the profound effect of the pandemic, economic problems, health challenges, adjusting to changing circumstances in your job, or helping a child who needs assistance with any number of things. Through change, we grow, learn, and adapt to the transitions in our lives. The quotes in this chapter offer perspective for making it through the most difficult times and sometimes encountering a "blessing in disguise" along the way.

Change is inevitable, growth is intentional.

—GLENDA CLOUD

All things change, and we change with them.

—MATTHIAS BORBONIUS

The only way to make sense out of change
is to plunge into it, move with it, and join the dance.

—ALAN WATTS

42

Change will not come if we wait for some other person or some
other time. We are the ones we've been waiting for.
We are the change that we seek.

—BARACK OBAMA

The secret of change is to focus all your energy,
not on fighting the old, but on building the new.

—DAN MILLMAN

The changes we dread most may contain our salvation.

—BARBARA KINGSOLVER

When we are no longer able to change a situation,
we are challenged to change ourselves.

—VIKTOR FRANKL

We must be the change we wish to see in the world.

—MAHATMA GANDHI

The world changes when we change.
The world softens when we soften.
The world loves us when we choose to love the world.

—MARIANNE WILLIAMSON

Change always comes bearing gifts.

—PRICE PRITCHETT

Not everything that is faced can be changed.
But nothing can be changed until it is faced.

—JAMES BALDWIN

Children

The joy of being a parent or an aunt or uncle brings so much depth to our lives. Children everywhere offer us this depth and perspective when we engage with them. It is the joy and wonder in a child's eyes as they perceive the world around them without judgment that gives me the most hope for the future. I love to talk with children, and look them in the eyes—I always find that I can catch some of their enthusiasm. Now, just to keep it!

You are the bows from which your children
as living arrows are sent forth.

—KAHLIL GIBRAN

Children are not only innocent and curious but also optimistic
and joyful and essentially happy. They are, in short, everything
adults wish they could be.

—CAROLYN HAYWOOD

Two of the greatest gifts we can give our children
are roots and wings.

—HODDING CARTER

Children are the living messages
we send to a time we will not see.

—NEIL POSTMAN

It is not what you do for your children, but what you have
taught them to do for themselves, that will make them
successful human beings.

—ANN LANDERS

Live so that when your children think of fairness, caring,
and integrity, they think of you.

—H. Jackson Brown Jr.

A new baby is like the beginning of all things—
wonder, hope, a dream of possibilities.

—Eda LeShan

To nourish children and raise them against odds is in any time,
any place, more valuable than to fix bolts in cars
or design nuclear weapons.

—Marilyn French

Each day of our lives we make deposits
in the memory banks of our children.

—Charles R. Swindoll

Your greatest contribution...may not be something you do,
but someone you raise.

—Andy Stanley

If I had influence with the good fairy who is supposed to preside over the christening of all children, I should ask that her gift to each child in the world be a sense of wonder so indestructible that it would last throughout life.

—RACHEL CARSON

The best thing to spend on your children is your time.

—LOUISE HART

Life is a flame that is always burning itself out, but it catches fire again every time a child is born.

—GEORGE BERNARD SHAW

While we try to teach our children all about life, our children teach us what life is about.

—ANGELA SCHWINDT

Don't worry that children never listen to you; worry that they are always watching you.

—ROBERT FULGHUM

48

Every child deserves a champion:
an adult who will never give up on them,
who understands the power of connection
and insists they become the best they can possibly be.

—RITA PIERSON

Children will listen to you
after they feel listened to.

—JANE NELSON

Children see magic because they look for it.

—CHRISTOPHER MOORE

Choices

How do we know what is the right choice at any given moment (especially when there are several possibilities)? The only way to know for sure is to choose and then find out where our journey takes us. Some people have a hunch or an instinct about the choices presented and know right away what to do. Other people gain great value in slowly exploring the options—maybe going as far as to make a pros and cons list; many people probably do both. Whichever way suits you, these quotes will give your thinking process (and your gut instincts) some added perspective. Just having the opportunity to choose is a blessing.

The hardest thing on earth is choosing what matters.

—SUE MONK KIDD

Do the right thing, in the right way, at the right time,
and for the right reasons.

—AUTHOR UNKNOWN

You have to leave the city of your comfort and go into the
wilderness of your intuition. You can't get there by bus, only by
hard work and risk and by not quite knowing what you're doing,
but what you'll discover will be wonderful. What you'll discover
will be yourself.

—ALAN ALDA

If you find yourself drawn to an event against all logic, go.
The universe is telling you something.

—GLORIA STEINEM

Ask yourself: What is the best I can do? And then do that.

—CHERYL STRAYED

52

Intentional living is the art of making our own choices before others' choices make us.

—Richie Norton

In life, you have three choices. Give up, give in, or give it your all.

—Charleston Parker

One's philosophy is not best expressed in words; it is expressed in the choices one makes. In the long run, we shape our lives and we shape ourselves. The process never ends until we die. And, the choices we make are ultimately our own responsibility.

—Eleanor Roosevelt

Choices can create momentum by launching a chain reaction—a series of events or feelings—whose impact is far greater than what you can foresee at the moment the choice is made.

—Tal Ben-Shahar

Understand that the right to choose your own path is a sacred privilege. Use it. Dwell in possibilities.

—Oprah Winfrey

I get up every morning determined to both change the world and have one hell of a good time. Sometimes this makes planning my day difficult.

—E. B. White

No matter what, we always have the power to choose hope over despair, engagement over apathy, kindness over indifference, love over hate.

—Cory Booker

At every moment in my life I have a choice. Moments add up to a lifetime; choices add up to a life.

—Tal Ben-Shahar

Comfort

There are times in which every person needs comfort, especially when dealing with loss, pain, and overbearing challenges. We need to be reminded that everyone faces loss—and they, too, have found ways to get through their most difficult periods. Many of us need affirmations that help guide us, which you'll find in this chapter.

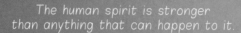

*The human spirit is stronger
than anything that can happen to it.*

—C. C. Scott

*While we cry ourselves to sleep, gratitude waits patiently to
console and reassure us; there is a landscape larger than the
one we can see.*

—Sarah Ban Breathnach

Move out of your comfort zone. You can only grow if you are
willing to feel awkward and uncomfortable
when you try something new.

—Brian Tracy

*You can't calm the storm, so stop trying.
What you can do is calm yourself.
The storm will pass.*

—Timber Hawkeye

Remember we all stumble, every one of us.
That's why it's a comfort to go hand in hand.

—Emily Kimbrough

56

I do not understand the mystery of grace—
only that it meets us where we are
and does not leave us where it found us.

—ANNE LAMOTT

The heart that breaks open can contain the whole universe.

—JOANNA MACY

When someone leaves you, let them go.
Their part in the story of your life may be over;
But your story goes on.

—KAREN SALMANSOHN

You are never alone or helpless.
The force that guides the stars guides you, too.

—SHRII SHRII ANANDAMURTI

Community

Helping others starts when we are children, whether it's helping a family member or a friend. By the time one reaches high school, a student can join one of a number of service clubs (and some children start much earlier, such as raising money for an important cause). From there, students are exposed to a broader outreach, such as marching for peace and justice. I hope the quotes here will inspire adults so they, in turn, can inspire their children. For every significant positive change in human history, it takes a community to make it happen. It is community that ties our achievements together and gives them meaning.

*I believe the world is one big family,
and we need to help each other.*

—Jet Li

*Connect deeply with others.
Our humanity is the one thing that we all have in common.*

—Melinda Gates

The best thing to hold onto in life is each other.

—Audrey Hepburn

60

*Care. Love. Be outraged. Be devastated.
Just don't give up.
The world needs good humans today.*

—Ellen DeGeneres

*The greatness of a community is most accurately measured by
the compassionate actions of its members, a heart of grace,
and a soul generated by love.*

—Coretta Scott King

Alone, we can do so little;
together, we can do so much.

—HELEN KELLER

In every community, there is work to be done.
In every nation, there are wounds to heal.
In every heart, there is the power to do it.

—MARIANNE WILLIAMSON

In the course of your lives, without any plan on your part,
you'll come to see suffering that will break your heart. When
it happens, and it will, don't turn away from it; turn toward it.
That is the moment when change is born.

—MELINDA GATES

If you want to go quickly, go alone.
If you want to go far, go together.

—AFRICAN PROVERB

Compassion

The thing about compassion is we're forever learning how to be better at it. One hears the phrase "practicing compassion," and that's the real truth of the idea. It's a practice, to be aware of those around you, and to think about what they need in this moment.

You can never know how many lives you've touched, so just know it's far more than you think. Even the tiniest acts of love, kindness, and compassion can have a massive ripple effect.

—LORI DESCHENE

God, teach us to carry each other
And know the lightness that comes with
Each step when it is taken with another.

—CORRINE DE WINTER

Encourage, lift, and strengthen one another. For the positive energy spread to one will be felt by us all.
For we are connected, one and all.

—DEBORAH DAY

No one is useless in the world
who lightens the burden of it for anyone else.

—CHARLES DICKENS

Too often we underestimate the power of a touch, a smile, a kind word, a listening ear, an honest compliment, or the smallest act of caring, all of which have the potential to turn a life around.

—LEO BUSCAGLIA

Compassion matters. It starts with you, it spreads to those around you, and then to the whole planet.

—KINARI WEBB

65

If you want others to be happy, practice compassion. If you want to be happy, practice compassion.

—H. H. DALAI LAMA

Sometimes our light goes out but is blown into flame by another human being. Each of us owes deepest thanks to those who have rekindled this light.

—ALBERT SCHWEITZER

What do we live for
if not to make life less difficult for each other?

—GEORGE ELIOT

The whole idea of compassion is based on a keen awareness
of the interdependence of all these living beings, which are all
part of one another, and all involved in one another.

—THOMAS MERTON

Compassion is not religious business, it is human business, it is
not luxury, it is essential for its own peace and mental stability,
it is essential for human survival.

—H. H. DALAI LAMA

We're all just walking each other home.

—RAM DASS

Courage

When we think of courage, historical figures such as Mahatma Gandhi, Marsha P. Johnson, Dr. Martin Luther King, Jr., Susan B. Anthony, Nelson Mandela, and Rosa Parks come to mind—as well as young people such as climate activist Greta Thunberg and the gun control activists from Marjory Stoneman Douglas High School. Each of these people acted with moral strength to persevere in the face of danger and opposition. Courage is what keeps us moving through difficulties or nudges us to try something new. It's the voice in our head that tells us it's okay to be uncomfortable in this moment. These quotes help lead the way toward becoming a more courageous person.

Don't wish me happiness. I don't expect to be happy all the time.... It's gotten beyond that, somehow. Wish me courage and strength and a sense of humor. I will need them all.

—ANNE MORROW LINDBERGH

We don't develop courage by being happy every day. We develop it by surviving difficult times and challenging adversity.

—BARBARA DE ANGELIS

Courage is not the absence of fear, but the capacity to act despite our fears.

—JOHN MCCAIN

68

If you want something you've never had before, you must do something you've never done before.

—AUTHOR UNKNOWN

You gain strength, courage and confidence by every experience in which you really stop to look fear in the face. You must do the thing you think you cannot do.

—ELEANOR ROOSEVELT

The most courageous act is to think for yourself. Aloud.

—COCO CHANEL

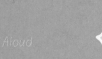

Courage doesn't always roar. Sometimes courage is the quiet voice at the end of the day saying, "I will try again tomorrow."

—MARY ANNE RADMACHER

Life shrinks or expands in proportion to one's courage.

—ANAÏS NIN

We were scared,
but our fear was not as strong as our courage.

—MALALA YOUSAFZAI

Courage is as contagious as fear.

—SUSAN SONTAG

69

I am stronger than I am broken.

—ROXANE GAY

To dare is to lose one's footing momentarily.
Not to dare is to lose oneself.

—SØREN KIERKEGAARD

To avoid criticism, do nothing, say nothing, be nothing.

—ELBERT HUBBARD

And the day came when the risk to remain tight in a bud
was more painful than the risk it took to blossom.

—ANAÏS NIN

It takes courage to grow up and become who you really are.

—E. E. CUMMINGS

70

The only courage that matters
is the kind that gets you from one moment to the next.

—MIGNON MCLAUGHLIN

Have patience with everything unresolved in your heart.

—RAINER MARIA RILKE

Overcome fear, behold wonder.

—RICHARD BACH

Creativity

Developing creative thinking skills can inspire and spark imagination and problem-solving in any area of life including business, the creative arts, home improvement, parenting, gardening, and self-discovery. Creative thinking is the ability to come up with fresh ideas and approach problems with a new perspective. It helps one see one's life through a focused lens of learning to pay attention to links, opposites, and juxtapositions, as well as shapes, colors, patterns, and textures. Playing around with new ideas is also a lot of fun!

Write it. Shoot it. Publish it. Crochet it, sauté it, whatever.
MAKE.

—Joss Whedon

Create. Not for the money. Not for the fame. Not for the
recognition. But for the pure joy of creating something
and sharing it.

—Ernest Barbaric

Not all of us are painters, but we are all artists.
Each time we fit things together we are creating.

—Corita Kent

If you hear a voice within you say, "you cannot paint,"
then by all means paint and that voice will be silenced.

—Vincent van Gogh

Creativity is the ability to pull things out of one's self or the
universe or wherever you think this stuff comes from,
and give it shape and form.

—Wendy Hale Davis

Art is when you hear a knocking from your soul—
and you answer.

—TERRI GUILLEMETS

Nothing feeds the center of being so much as creative work.

—ANNE MORROW LINDBERGH

Consider everything an experiment.

—CORITA KENT

Live the full life of the mind, exhilarated by new ideas,
intoxicated by the Romance of the unusual.

—ERNEST HEMINGWAY

And suddenly you know...
it's time to start something new
and trust the magic of new beginnings.

—MEISTER ECKHART

To practice any art, no matter how well or badly,
is a way to make your soul grow. So do it.

—KURT VONNEGUT

*Creativity is inventing, experimenting, growing, taking risks,
breaking rules, making mistakes, and having fun.*

—MARY LOU COOK

*Creativity involves breaking out of expected patterns
in order to look at things in a different way.*

—EDWARD DE BONO

*You can't wait for inspiration,
you have to go after it with a club.*

—JACK LONDON

*Creativity is just connecting things. When you ask creative
people how they did something, they feel a little guilty because
they didn't really do it, they just saw something.
It seemed obvious to them after a while.*

—STEVE JOBS

*All life is an experiment.
The more experiments you make, the better.*

—RALPH WALDO EMERSON

Expose yourself to as much randomness as possible. Attend conferences no one else is attending. Read books no one else is reading. Talk to people no one else is talking to.

—BEN CASNOCHA

If you don't make space for creativity to grow and thrive, it will get stomped out by all the to-dos.

—ERIN BENZAKEIN

If you can see yourself as an artist, and you can see that your life is your own creation, then why not create the most beautiful story for yourself?

—MIGUEL RUIZ

Make visible what, without you, might perhaps never have been seen.

—ROBERT BRESSON

Nonsense and beauty have close connections.

—E. M. FORSTER

So you see, imagination needs moodling—
long, inefficient, happy idling, dawdling, and puttering.

—Brenda Ueland

What if imagination and art are not frosting at all,
but the fountainhead of human experience?

—Rollo May

One of the advantages of being disorderly
is that one is constantly making exciting discoveries.

—A. A. Milne

The best way to have a good idea
is to have lots of ideas.

—Linus Pauling

You can't use up creativity.
The more you use, the more you have.

—Maya Angelou

Dreams

So you want to pursue your dreams? Or expand on the ones you've already achieved? The quotes here will offer you motivation and many ideas. Every person's journey is filled with dreams, each of which has the potential to change your life—or even change the world. We will never know what we might achieve unless we dream about the possibilities, pursue our aspirations, and stay determined.

Every great dream begins with a dreamer. Always remember,
you have within you the strength, the patience, and the passion
to reach for the stars to change the world.

—AUTHOR UNKNOWN

What would you attempt to do if you knew you could not fail?

—ROBERT H. SCHULLER

You see things; and say "Why?"
But I dream things that never were; and I say, "Why not?"

—GEORGE BERNARD SHAW

Throw your dreams into space like a kite, and you do not know
what it will bring back, a new life, a new friend, a new love,
a new country.

—ANAÏS NIN

When I reach the place of my dreams,
I will thank my failures and tears. They too, kept me going.

—DODINSKY

They only shot a body but they cannot shoot my dreams.

—MALALA YOUSAFZAI

Instead of looking at the past, I put myself ahead twenty
years and try to look at what I need to do now
in order to get there then.

—DIANA ROSS

I dream. I plan. I act.

—JANE POLLAK

Cherish your visions and your dreams as they are the children
of your soul, the blueprints of your ultimate achievements.

—NAPOLEON HILL

The size of your dreams must always exceed your current capacity to achieve them. If your dreams do not scare you, they are not big enough.

—Ellen Johnson Sirleaf

Never be limited by other people's limited imagination.

—Mae Jemison

The more you can dream, the more you can do.

—Michael Korda

Whatever you can do, or dream you can, begin it. Boldness has genius, power, and magic in it.

—Johann Wolfgang von Goethe

To accomplish great things, we must not only act, but also dream.

—Anatole France

Whatever you're thinking, think bigger.

—TONY HSIEH

*Tell me, what do you plan to do
with your one wild and precious life?*

—MARY OLIVER

If there were dreams to sell, what would you buy?

—THOMAS BEDDOES

*Never, never rest contented with any circle of ideas,
but always be certain that a wider one is still possible.*

—PEARL BAILEY

*Look at the sky. We are not alone. The whole universe is
friendly to us and conspires only to give the best
to those who dream and work.*

—A. P. J. ABDUL KALAM

Don't let anyone build your world for you.
They always build it too small.

—HOLLY DEAN

The morning's the size of heaven. What will you do with it?

—MARK DOTY

"One can't believe impossible things," Alice said. "I daresay you haven't had much practice," said the Queen. "When I was your age, I always did it for half an hour a day. Why, sometimes I've believed as many as six impossible things before breakfast."

—LEWIS CARROLL

I believe that every life is valuable. That we can make things better. That innovation is the key to a bright future. That we're just getting started.

—BILL GATES

It's always within yourself that you find the strength to dance the steps you've dreamed.

—LAURA JEAN JUDSON

82

Faith

Faith is complete trust or confidence in something. Learning how to have faith is a journey we all traverse throughout our lives; it becomes the ability to accept the uncertainty of the moment while still believing in the moment after this one. This chapter shares the wisdom of souls who spent their lives learning how to have faith.

Faith is taking the first step
even when you don't see the whole staircase.

—DR. MARTIN LUTHER KING JR.

My heart holds my faith— my spirit, its strength.

—JUNE COTNER

The dark night of the soul comes just before revelation.

—JOSEPH CAMPBELL

Every tomorrow has two handles. We can take hold of it
with the handle of anxiety or the handle of faith.

—HENRY WARD BEECHER

There isn't enough room in your mind for both worry and faith.
You must decide which one will live there.

—SIR WILLIAM ROBERTSON

Embrace uncertainty. Some of the most beautiful chapters
in our lives won't have a title until much later.

—BOB GOFF

*Sometimes when you're in a dark place,
you think you've been buried, but you've actually been planted.*

—Christine Caine

*If you believe it will work out, you'll see opportunities.
If you believe it won't, you will see obstacles.*

—Wayne Dyer

*The only way we can change the way we feel is by becoming
aware of our inner experience and learning to befriend
what is going inside ourselves.*

—Bessel van der Kolk

*Surrender to what is, let go of what was,
have faith in what will be.*

—Sonia Ricotti

*Faith is the bird that feels the light
and sings when the dawn is still and dark.*

—Rabindranath Tagore

85

I have one life and one chance to make it count for something.
My faith demands that I do whatever I can, wherever I am,
whenever I can, for as long as I can with whatever I have to
try to make a difference.

—JIMMY CARTER

Faith is believing in the possibility that whatever happens is
happening to us for a reason. The things that come into our
lives are either blessings or they carry great lessons.
Faith is believing in this.

—MEGAN MURPHY

For we walk by faith, not by sight.

—2 CORINTHIANS 5:7

Faith is a willingness to take the next step,
to see the unknown as an adventure, to launch a journey.

—SHARON SALZBERG

Family

The best thing about family is that it can encompass not only those related to you by genes but also those whom you choose to be a part of your family. They are your support system and offer unconditional love and acceptance. They are your companions along the path we take through life.

In every conceivable manner,
the family is link to our past, bridge to our future.

—ALEX HALEY

Parenthood: it's about guiding the next generation
and forgiving the last.

—PETER KRAUSE

It's family and friends who pick us up when we fall down.
And if they can't pick us up, they lie down next to us
and just listen and love.

—ANDI DORFMAN

Home should be an anchor, a port in a storm, a refuge,
a happy place in which to dwell, a place where we are loved
and where we can love.

—MARVIN J. ASHTON

Families are like branches on a tree—
we grow in different directions
yet our roots remain as one.

—AUTHOR UNKNOWN

Your parents miss you and wish you'd call.
Later you'll miss them and wish you could.

—PAUL GRAHAM

Grandchildren are the dots that connect the lines
from generation to generation.

—LOIS WYSE

Families are the compass that guides us.
They are the inspiration to reach great heights,
and our comfort when we occasionally falter.

—BRAD HENRY

89

Treat your family like friends and your friends like family.

—AUTHOR UNKNOWN

Call it a clan, call it a network, call it a tribe, call it a family.
Whatever you call it, whoever you are, you need one.

—JANE HOWARD

Family isn't about whose blood you have.
It's about who you care about.

—TREY PARKER AND MATT STONE

Family is not an important thing—it's everything.

—Michael J. Fox

Families are ecosystems.
Each life grows in response to the lives around it.

—Mary Schmich

You don't choose your family.
They are God's gift to you, as you are to them.

—Archbishop Desmond Tutu

Cherish every moment with those you love
at every stage of your journey.

—Jack Layton

Fatherhood

The fathers in this chapter tell us how unique the role of fatherhood is in the life of a child. In reading this chapter, you'll be exposed to developing patience and kindness and becoming aware of your child in relation to their surroundings. Every individual's story is distinct, and being a father is something every father learns how to do through a unique lens. The common theme through all of these voices is love.

It is not biology that determines fatherhood. It is love.

—KRISTIN HANNAH

Every dad, if he takes time out of his busy life to reflect upon his fatherhood, can learn ways to become an even better dad.

—JACK BAKER

My father didn't tell me how to live.
He lived and let me watch him do it.

—CLARENCE BUDINGTON KELLAND

My father gave me the greatest gift anyone could give another person, he believed in me.

—JIM VALVANO

Anyone who tells you fatherhood is the greatest thing that can happen to you, they are understating it.

—MIKE MYERS

Fatherhood didn't just happen to me.
I am deliberately living it, reimagining it, and rediscovering it
every day. It is as beautiful as I make it,
just like anything else in life.

—Hrithik Roshan

Real fatherhood means love and commitment and sacrifice and
a willingness to share responsibility and not walking away
from one's family.

—William Bennett

If there is any immortality to be had among us human beings, it
is certainly only in the love that we leave behind.
Fathers like mine don't ever die.

—Leo Buscaglia

Forgiveness

In deciding whether to forgive someone, a person experiences a change in feelings about an offense, whether it was large or small. The forgiver is able to overcome negative emotions such as resentment. While forgiving can be challenging, one's capacity to forgive is also a recognition of the strengths we are capable of developing. Our capacity for kindness grows immensely through forgiveness. After forgiving someone, we realize that forgiveness is a gift that lightens our own spirit.

Forgiveness doesn't make the other person right,
it makes you free.

—STORMIE OMARTIAN

Those who cannot forgive others break the bridge
over which they themselves must pass.

—CONFUCIUS

To err is human; to forgive, divine.

—ALEXANDER POPE

The weak can never forgive
Forgiveness is an attribute of the strong.

—MAHATMA GANDHI

The only way out of the labyrinth of suffering is to forgive.

—JOHN GREEN

To forgive is to set a prisoner free
and realize that prisoner was you

—LEWIS B. SMEDES

Forgive yourself for not knowing better at the time. Forgive yourself for giving away your power. Forgive yourself for past behaviors. Forgive yourself for the survival patterns and traits you picked up while enduring trauma. Forgive yourself for being who you needed to be.

—AUDREY KITCHING

Weigh the true advantages of forgiveness and resentment to the heart. Then choose.

—JACK KORNFIELD

Forgiveness is the fragrance the violet sheds on the heel that has crushed it.

—MARK TWAIN

Forgive, forget, and forge ahead.

—AUTHOR UNKNOWN

True forgiveness is not an action after the fact, it is an attitude with which you enter each moment.

—DAVID RIDGE

Friendship

Where would we be without our friends? I am especially grateful for friends who live far away—and when we get together, we can pick up where we left off. Time doesn't erase the bond of mutual affection and support. Our friends have our backs; they have our best interest at heart. We, in turn, offer reciprocal love and support—we cherish the bond of friendship and grow deeper in love with them.

*We are all travelers in the wilderness of this world,
and the best we can find in our travels is an honest friend.*

—ROBERT LOUIS STEVENSON

*Sitting silently beside a friend who is hurting
may be the best gift we can give.*

—AUTHOR UNKNOWN

*The most beautiful discovery true friends make
is that they can grow separately without growing apart.*

—ELIZABETH FOLEY

*A friend knows the song in my heart
and sings it to me when my memory fails.*

—DONNA ROBERTS

Friends are the family we choose for ourselves.

—EDNA BUCHANAN

*That is the best—to laugh with someone
because you both think the same things are funny.*

—GLORIA VANDERBILT

The most ordinary things could be made extraordinary,
simply by doing them with the right people.

—NICHOLAS SPARKS

When you're with a friend, your heart has come home.

—EMILY FARRAR

We need old friends to help us grow old
and new friends to help us stay young.

—LETTY COTTIN POGREBIN

My friends are my estate.

—EMILY DICKINSON

There's no word for old friends who've just met.

—JIM HENSON

Wherever you are, it's your friends who make your world.

—WILLIAM JAMES

Friendships double our joys and divide our griefs.

—SWEDISH PROVERB

Life's truest happiness is found in friendships
we make along the way.

—Author unknown

Each friend represents a world in us, a world possibly not born
until they arrive, and it is only by this meeting
that a new world is born.

—Anaïs Nin

Friendship is born at that moment when one person says to
another: "What! You too? I thought I was the only one."

—C. S. Lewis

102

Oh, the comfort, the inexpressible comfort of feeling safe
with a person; having neither to weigh thoughts nor measure
words, but to pour them all out, just as they are, chaff and
grain together, knowing that a faithful hand will take and sift
them, keep what is worth keeping, and then, with a breath of
kindness, blow the rest away.

—Dinah Maria Mulock Craik

A friend is someone who understands your past, believes in
your future, and accepts you the way you are.

—Author unknown

You can make more friends in two months by becoming
interested in other people than you can in two years by trying
to get other people interested in you.

—Dale Carnegie

A friend is the one who comes in
when the whole world has gone out.

—Grace Pulpit

103

In prosperity, our friends know us;
in adversity, we know our friends.

—John Churton Collins

Friends—they cherish one another's hopes.
They are kin to one another's dreams.

—Henry David Thoreau

Gratitude

I was particularly grateful when gratitude journals started being published about ten years ago. I find they are a great way to add a positive lens through which I view the world. The more things I identify to appreciate, the more I see a universe of gratitude around me. I hope you will become a "noticer" of people and surroundings that delight you. The selections in this chapter will encourage you to pay attention to things that make you laugh, the places that nourish you, the loved ones who inspire and guide you, and caring strangers who bring blessings to your days.

Acknowledging the good that you already have in your life is the foundation for all abundance.

—ECKHART TOLLE

Just to be is a blessing. Just to live is holy.

—RABBI ABRAHAM JOSHUA HESCHEL

Give thanks for unknown blessings already on their way.

—NATIVE AMERICAN PROVERB

When you arise in the morning, give thanks for the morning light, for your life and strength. Give thanks for your food and the joy of living. If you see no reason for giving thanks, the fault lies with yourself.

—CHIEF TECUMSEH

I opened two gifts this morning. They were my eyes.

—ZIG ZIGLAR

For all that has been—thanks. For all that shall be—yes.

—DAG HAMMARKSJÖLD

There are hundreds of ways to kneel and kiss the ground.

—RUMI

If the only prayer you ever say in your entire life
is thank you, it will be enough.

—MEISTER ECKHART

Be thankful for what you have; you'll end up having more.
If you concentrate on what you don't have,
you will never, ever have enough.

—OPRAH WINFREY

The most fortunate are those who have a wonderful capacity
to appreciate again and again, freshly and naively, the basic
goods of life, with awe, pleasure, wonder, and even ecstasy.

—ABRAHAM MASLOW

Be glad of life because it gives you the chance to love
and to work and to play and to look up at the stars.

—HENRY VAN DYKE

Blessings brighten when we count them.

—MALTBIE DAVENPORT BABCOCK

*A thankful heart is not only the greatest virtue,
but the parent of all virtues.*

—CICERO

*In ordinary life we hardly realize that we receive a great deal
more than we give, and that it is only with gratitude that life
becomes rich.*

—DIETRICH BONHOEFFER

Praise the bridge that carried you over.

—GEORGE COLMAN

*Gratitude as a discipline involves a conscious choice. I can
choose to be grateful even when my emotions and feelings are
still steeped in hurt and resentment. It is amazing how many
occasions present themselves in which I can choose gratitude
instead of a complaint.*

—HENRI J. M. NOUWEN

We can only be said to be alive in those moments
when our hearts are conscious of our treasures.

—THORNTON WILDER

Let gratitude in the evening
bring you joy in the morning.

—JUNE COTNER

Each day comes
bearing its own gifts.
Untie the ribbons.

—RUTH ANN SCHABACKER

Grieving

Grieving is as much a part of life as falling in love or giving birth. Often, it comes at unexpected times and becomes our natural response to deep loss. We feel intense sorrow and can't imagine how we will learn to live and adapt to the pain of knowing this person isn't with us on earth. Some people find a lot of comfort in visualizing loved ones as guardian angels in their lives. Whether your grief is new or years old, I hope these quotes will offer you some solace.

Though nothing can bring back the hour
Of splendour in the grass, of glory in the flower;
We will grieve not, rather find
Strength in what remains behind...

—WILLIAM WORDSWORTH

...even out of unspeakable grief, beautiful things take wing.

—A. R. TORRES

Grief, I've learned, is really just love. It's all the love you
want to give but cannot. All that unspent love gathers up in
the corners of your eyes, the lump in your throat, and in that
hollow part of your chest. Grief is just love with no place to go.

—JAMIE ANDERSON

There are stars whose radiance is visible on Earth though
they have long been extinct. There are people whose brilliance
continues to light the world even though they are no longer
among the living. These lights are particularly bright when the
night is dark. They light the way for humankind.

—HANNAH SZENES

112

Perhaps they are not stars in the sky, but rather openings
where our loved ones shine down to let us know they are happy.

—AUTHOR UNKNOWN

I know now that we never get over great losses; we absorb
them, and they carve us into different, often kinder, creatures.

—GAIL CALDWELL

113

Grief is in two parts.
The first is loss.
The second is the remaking of life.

—ANNE ROIPHE

There is grace in grief
and strength in sorrow.

—ANNIE DOUGHERTY

From moment to moment one can bear much.

—TERESA OF AVILA

Though much is taken, much abides…

—ALFRED LORD TENNYSON

The most beautiful people are those who have known defeat,
known suffering, known struggle, known loss, and have
found their way out of the depths. These persons have an
appreciation, a sensitivity, and an understanding of life that
fills them with compassion, gentleness,
and a deep loving concern.

—ELISABETH KÜBLER-ROSS

Between grief and nothing, I will take grief.

—WILLIAM FAULKNER

Growth

Life is constant growth. Just consider time-lapse photography, in which you can view a flower bud coming into full bloom. Our lives are like that, too—always growing—but we're more inclined to resist growth because we aren't ready for it—or we see growth as negative. In developing a growth-oriented mindset, the quotes in this chapter will provide a lot of encouragement.

In any given moment we have two options:
to step forward into growth or to step back into safety.

—ABRAHAM MASLOW

When life is sweet, say thank you and celebrate.
When life is bitter, say thank you and grow.

—SHAUNA NIEQUIST

When something bad happens, you have three choices.
You can let it define you, let it destroy you,
or you can let it strengthen you.

—DR. SEUSS

If you are going through a time of discouragement,
there is a time of great personal growth ahead.

—OSWALD CHAMBERS

When you can't go far, you go deep.

—BROTHER DAVID STEINDL-RAST

Action brings with it its own courage, its own energy, a growth
of self-confidence that can be acquired in no other way.

—ELEANOR ROOSEVELT

I learned to always take on things I'd never done before.
Growth and comfort do not coexist.

—GINNI ROMETTY

Because things are the way they are,
things will not stay the way they are.

—BERTOLT BRECHT

You cannot help to build a better world without improving
individually. To that end each of us must work
for his own improvement.

—MARIE CURIE

When you plant a seed that is love, it is you that blossoms.

—MA JAYA SATI BHAGAVATI

As human beings, our greatness lies not so much in being able
to remake the world—that is the myth of the "atomic age"—
as in being able to remake ourselves.

—MAHATMA GANDHI

Every blade of grass has an angel that bends over it
and whispers, "Grow! Grow!"

—THE TALMUD

Happiness

What is happiness? We know when we're feeling it because we're experiencing pleasure, joy, and often bliss. Happiness is a state of mind that is created from within. While big achievements will bring you some happiness, it's often the little things which can bring you the greatest happiness. Having a positive frame of mind and taking the opportunity to do what you love are two of the keys to increasing happiness. In addition, the quotes here offer a variety of ideas for creating a pathway toward more happiness in your life.

Be happy for this moment. This moment is your life.

—OMAR KHAYYAM

Happiness cannot be traveled to, owned, earned, worn, or
consumed. Happiness is the spiritual experience
of living every minute with love, grace, and gratitude.

—DENIS WAITLEY

Rules for happiness:
something to do, someone to love, something to hope for.

—IMMANUEL KANT

Of this to be sure: You do not find the happy life—you make it.

—THOMAS S. MONSON

Why not seize the pleasure at once? —How often is happiness
destroyed by preparation, foolish preparation!

—JANE AUSTEN

It is sweet to be silly at the right moment.

—HORACE

Remember that the happiest people are not those getting more,
but those giving more.

—H. JACKSON BROWN JR. AND ROCHELLE PENNINGTON

Some people pursue happiness, others create it.

—RALPH WALDO EMERSON

Happiness is not a station you arrive at,
but a manner of traveling.

—MARGARET LEE RUNBECK

We didn't realize we were making memories,
we just knew we were having fun.

—A. A. MILNE, *WINNIE THE POOH*

Let us be grateful to people who make us happy;
they are the charming gardeners who make our souls blossom.

—MARCEL PROUST

It is not how much we have,
but how much we enjoy, that makes happiness.

—CHARLES SPURGEON

Judge nothing, you will be happy.
Forgive everything, you will be happier.
Love everything, you will be happiest.

—SRI CHINMOY

Thousands of candles can be lighted from a single candle,
and the life of the candle will not be shortened.
Happiness never decreases by being shared.

—THE BUDDHA

Happiness, not in another place but this place...
not for another hour, but this hour.

—WALT WHITMAN

Health

We're each in charge of our health—the melding of physical and emotional well-being. While many of us focus on creating a healthy lifestyle starting with the new year, there's nothing to prevent you from doing so today. The thoughts in this chapter are easy and simple. They provide excellent affirmations for improving one's health.

The first wealth is health.

—RALPH WALDO EMERSON

Take care of your body. It's the only place you have to live.

—JIM ROHN

A healthy mind does not speak ill of others.

—AUTHOR UNKNOWN

It is health that is real wealth
and not pieces of gold and silver.

—MAHATMA GANDHI

124

A fit body, a calm mind, a house full of love.
These things cannot be bought—they must be earned.

—NAVAL RAVIKANT

The wound is the place where light enters you.

—RUMI

There is no medicine like hope, no incentive so great, and no
tonic so powerful as expectation of something tomorrow.

—ORISON SWETT MARDEN

Those who think they have no time for healthy eating
will sooner or later have to find time for illness.

—EDWARD STANLEY

Health is the greatest gift,
contentment the greatest wealth,
faithfulness the best relationship.

—THE BUDDHA

Laughter is inner jogging.

—NORMAN COUSINS

Calm mind brings inner strength and self-confidence,
so that's very important for good health.

—H. H. DALAI LAMA

In order to truly give to others,
you have to give to yourself first.

—ALI VINCENT

A good laugh and a long sleep
are the best cures in the doctor's book.

—IRISH PROVERB

Hope

Hope is having a positive attitude about the circumstances in one's life—along with the belief that an undesired situation will improve. Hope can also be more upbeat—such as wishing that a certain team wins, that you receive a scholarship, or that your dream vacation becomes a reality. Let these quotes remind you that hope is a stepping-stone to the next happiness in your life.

Hope is not a resting place but a starting point...

—H. Jackson Brown Jr.

Each dawn holds a new hope for a new plan.

—Gina Blair

*Never give up hope. All things are working for your good.
One day, you'll look back on everything you've been through
and thank God for it.*

—Germany Kent

In all things it is better to hope than to despair.

—Johann Wolfgang von Goethe

*We must accept finite disappointment,
but never lose infinite hope.*

—Dr. Martin Luther King Jr.

Hope is the belief that the darkness will change.

—Nancy Tupper Ling

Hope is the deep orientation of the human soul
that can be held at the darkest times.

—Vaclav Havel

Hope is being able to see that there is light
despite all of the darkness.

—Archbishop Desmond Tutu

I dwell in possibility.

—Emily Dickinson

129

Expect to have hope rekindled.
Expect your prayers to be
answered in wondrous ways.
The dry seasons in life do not last.
The spring rains will come again.

—Sarah Ban Breathnach

Hope is the thing with feathers
That perches in the soul—
And sings the tune without the words—
And never stops at all.

—Emily Dickinson

By nature we feel hope when tragedy occurs.
Hope is our instinct. Embrace it.

—KIRSTEN CASEY

Never give up, for that is just the place and time
that the tide will turn.

—HARRIET BEECHER STOWE

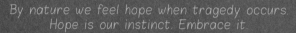

May we never give up hope, whatever the terrors, difficulties,
and obstacles that rise up against us. May those obstacles only
inspire us to even deeper determination. May we have faith in
the undying love and power of all the enlightened beings that
have blessed and still bless the earth with their presence. May
the visions of so many mystic masters of all traditions of a
future world free of cruelty and horror, where humanity can
live on earth in the ultimate joy of union,
be realized through all our efforts.

—ANDREW HARVEY

Individuality

Ahhh...individuality! What fun it is to figure out what makes you unique. What are the qualities that distinguish you from others? Some ways of expressing individuality include finding a hobby you love, dressing in a certain style, speaking out, and staying true to yourself. Maintaining one's identity can be a challenge when there are many conflicting voices in the world telling us to conform to someone else's vision or viewpoint. These quotes will encourage you to listen to your own voice.

The privilege of a lifetime is being who you are.

—JOSEPH CAMPBELL

Nothing can dim the light that shines from within.

—MAYA ANGELOU

By being yourself, you put something wonderful in the world
that was not there before.

—EDWIN ELLIOT

*Celebrate your humanness. Celebrate your craziness...
celebrate you.*

—LEO BUSCAGLIA

The great pleasure in life is doing
what people say you cannot do.

—WALTER BAGEHOT

Do you know what you are? You are a marvel.

—PABLO CASALS

Only in spontaneity can we be who we truly are.

—JOHN MCLAUGHLIN

There is only one you in all time.

—Martha Graham

Every individual matters.
Every individual has a role to play.
Every individual makes a difference.

—Jane Goodall

We have to dare to be ourselves,
however frightening or strange that self may prove to be.

—May Sarton

Our task is to say a holy yes
to the real things of our life as they exist—
the real truth of who we are.

—Natalie Goldberg

To be that self which one truly is.

—Søren Kierkegaard

Inspiration

A spark of inspiration can light up your imagination. And who knows what can come into being from that spark? Hold on to that inspiration; use it to fuel your passion and your goals. This chapter shares with us what can result from inspiration, and how to find it when we're not sure what path to take. Your inspiration could cause a domino effect of change, making a difference in the world you want to create.

If we all did things we are capable of doing,
we would literally astound ourselves.

—THOMAS EDISON

Act as if what you do makes a difference. It does.

—WILLIAM JAMES

Share your sparkle wherever you are.

—DODINSKY

136

Keep looking for new trouble.

—GEORGE CLOONEY

Live the way you want to be remembered.

—DILLON BURROUGHS

One moment can change a day, one day can change a life
and one life can change the world.

—THE BUDDHA

We have only this moment, sparkling like a star in our hand,
and melting like a snowflake.

—SIR FRANCIS BACON

Your time is limited.
So don't waste it living someone else's life.

—STEVE JOBS

Be humble for you are made of earth.
Be noble because you are made of stars.

—SERBIAN PROVERB

137

Above all, watch with glittering eyes the whole world around you
because the greatest secrets are always hidden in the most
unlikely places. Those who don't believe in magic
will never find it.

—ROALD DAHL

The best is yet to be.

—ROBERT BROWNING

Integrity

Act with integrity, and we will never regret how we act. Let these quotes remind you to choose honesty in all things, travel through your days with strong moral principles, be ethically solid, show respect to all, and convey true kindness. By our actions, we inspire others to do the same. If one can live as a person of integrity, they will have succeeded at changing the world for the better. These quotes, starting with the first one, will help anyone move toward becoming a person with true integrity.

Real integrity is doing the right thing, knowing that nobody's going to know whether you did it or not.

—OPRAH WINFREY

You teach people how to treat you by what you allow, what you stop, and what you reinforce.

—TONY A. GASKINS JR.

Before you speak, let your words pass through three gates:
"Is it true?
Is it necessary?
Is it kind?"

—SUFI SAYING

When people talk, listen completely. Most people never listen.

—ERNEST HEMINGWAY

With integrity, you have nothing to fear, since you have nothing to hide. With integrity, you will do the right thing, so you will have no guilt.

—ZIG ZIGLAR

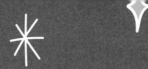

It's not the violence of the few that scares me,
it's the silence of the many.

—Dr. Martin Luther King Jr.

To give real service you must add something which cannot be
bought or measured with money,
and that is sincerity and integrity.

—Douglas Adams

One of the truest tests of integrity
is its blunt refusal to be compromised.

—Chinua Achebe

141

Whatever is true, whatever is honorable,
whatever is right, whatever is pure,
whatever is lovely, whatever is of good repute...
dwell on these things.

—Philippians 4:8

It is character that should be the sole measure of judgement
in the society of thinking humanity,
and nothing short of that would do.

—Abhijit Naskar

It is clear that the way to heal society of its violence...
and lack of love is to replace the pyramid of domination
with the circle of equality and respect.

—Manitonquat

Truth is powerful and it prevails.

—Sojourner Truth

Let us all hope that the dark clouds of racial prejudice will
soon pass away, and that in some not too distant tomorrow
the radiant stars of love and brotherhood will shine over our
great nation with all their scintillating beauty.

—Dr. Martin Luther King Jr.

Joy

Joy is a simple delight in the unexpected. It can also be cultivated. Some people even start a joy journal in which they record items such as things that made them laugh that day, thoughts about people they love, what they appreciate about others, places that give them peace, random happy thoughts, and things they love to do. You can look over the quotes here and even create a list of twenty things, people, or places that bring you joy.

It is not joy that makes us grateful;
it is gratitude that makes us joyful.

—BROTHER DAVID STEINDL-RAST

You're worried about how you're going to feel at the end of
your life? What about right now? Live. Right this minute.
That's where the joy's at.

—ABIGAIL THOMAS

Joy is what happens to us when we allow ourselves
to recognize how good things really are.

—MARIANNE WILLIAMSON

Joy does not simply happen to us.
We have to choose joy and keep choosing it every day.

—HENRI J. M. NOUWEN

*Love the moment, and the energy of that moment
will spread beyond all boundaries.*

—CORITA KENT

Things and conditions can give you pleasure but they cannot
give you joy—joy arises from within.

—ECKHART TOLLE

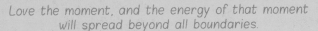

*The soul should always stand ajar, ready to welcome
the ecstatic experience.*

—EMILY DICKINSON

*O how I laugh when I think of my vague indefinite riches. No
run on my bank can drain it, for my wealth is not possession
but enjoyment.*

—HENRY DAVID THOREAU

The happiest people take responsibility
for creating their own joy.

—LORI DESCHENE

Sometimes your joy is the source of your smile, but sometimes
your smile can be the source of your joy.

—THÍCH NHẤT HẠNH

On with the dance! Let joy be unconfined.

—LORD BYRON

Kindness

Reading the quotes in this chapter is an encouraging reminder
that every person is on their own journey through life, and it
does me no harm to be kind to everyone. Kindness multiplies
exponentially and can be the one thing that makes someone
else's day better. How we make other people feel also has a
direct effect on how we ourselves feel. So why not spend each
moment of interaction kindly? It can have only a positive result

Be kind, for everyone you meet is fighting a hard battle.

—IAN MACLAREN

The smallest act of kindness is worth more
than the grandest intention.

—OSCAR WILDE

I've learned that people will forget what you said,
people will forget what you did, but people will never forget
how you made them feel.

—CARL W. BUEHNER

148

Beginning today, treat everyone you meet as if he or she were
going to be dead by midnight. Extend to them all the care,
kindness, and understanding you can muster, and do so with no
thought of any reward. Your life will never be the same.

—OG MANDINO

A warm smile is the universal language of kindness

—WILLIAM ARTHUR WARD

Err in the direction of kindness.

—GEORGE SAUNDERS

Kind words can be short and easy to speak,
but their echoes are truly endless.

—Blessed Mother Teresa

In life you can never be too kind or too fair; everyone you
meet is carrying a heavy load. When you go through your day
expressing kindness and courtesy to all you meet, you leave
behind a feeling of warmth and good cheer, and you help
alleviate the burdens everyone is struggling with.

—Brian Tracy

We won't always know whose lives we touched and made better
for our having cared, because actions can sometimes have
unforeseen ramifications. What's important is that you do care
and you act.

—Charlotte Lunsford

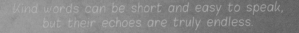

Leadership

Leadership is more than showing the way. Leadership is
listening and learning, trusting, and inspiring creativity. When
people believe in you, they start to follow. And that level of
responsibility is something to take seriously. I appreciate how
clearly the quotes in this chapter remind us that leadership
doesn't always consist of the things we first think of—leadership
is a trait one must develop over time.

If your actions inspire others to dream more, learn more,
do more, and become more, you are a leader.

—John Quincy Adams

When you can't find someone to follow,
you have to find a way to lead by example.

—Roxane Gay

A leader takes people where they want to go. A great leader
takes people where they don't necessarily want to go,
but ought to be.

—Rosalynn Carter

Never tell people how to do things. Tell them what to do
and they will surprise you with their ingenuity.

—George S. Patton Jr.

Example is not the main thing influencing others.
It is the only thing.

—ALBERT SCHWEITZER

Excellence is to do a common thing in an uncommon way.

—BOOKER T. WASHINGTON

Ability may get you to the top, but it takes character
to keep you there.

—JOHN WOODEN

You may have to fight a battle more than once to win it.

—MARGARET THATCHER

When they go low, we go high.

—MICHELLE OBAMA

153

Life

Life is a gift and a journey. When one's mind, heart, and soul is satisfied, life feels good. We recognize that the ups and downs are a part of life and this serves to make life interesting. The quotes in this chapter remind me that there is no time but the present to live—so take this moment and leap right into it! I encourage you to live fully and to act in such a way that all of us impact others positively. Hopefully we will be content with the life we have shaped when we have reached the end.

Life is not measured by the number of breaths we take,
but the moments that take our breath away.

—AUTHOR UNKNOWN

Do something today that your future self will thank you for.

—SEAN PATRICK FLANERY

If I had my life to live over,
I'd dare to make more mistakes next time.

—NADINE STAIR

Life is a great and wondrous mystery, and the only thing we
know that we have for sure is what is right here right now.
Don't miss it.

—LEO BUSCAGLIA

Life is a mystery to be lived, not a problem to be solved.

—ADRIANA TRIGIANI

Make a gift of your life and lift all...by being kind, considerate,
forgiving, and compassionate at all times, in all places, and
under all conditions, with everyone as well as yourself.
This is the greatest gift anyone can give.

—DAVID R. HAWKINS

Life itself is the most wonderful fairy tale.

—Hans Christian Andersen

*To be alive in this beautiful, self-organizing universe—
to participate in the dance of life with senses to perceive it,
lungs that breathe it, organs that draw nourishment from it—
is a wonder beyond words.*

—Joanna Macy and Molly Brown

*No matter where life takes you,
the place that you stand at any moment is holy ground.*

—Susan Vreeland

*Stay true to your deepest intuition
that an extraordinary and miraculous life is possible.*

—Craig Hamilton

*Life is no brief candle for me. It is a sort of splendid torch,
which I have got hold of for the moment, and I want to
make it burn as brightly as possible before handing it on to
future generations.*

—George Bernard Shaw

Life isn't about getting and having, it's about giving and being.

—KEVIN KRUSE

I don't want to get to the end of my life and find that I lived just the length of it. I want to have lived the width as well.

—DIANE ACKERMAN

Here's the question. What have I come here to do with my life? That's the question that begins every single quest.

—ELIZABETH GILBERT

The art of life is not controlling what happens, it's using what happens.

—GLORIA STEINEM

We have the choice to use the gift of our life to make the world a better place.

—JANE GOODALL

So, have fun. Get into your life and do what you enjoy and be the best at what you can be. Maybe you won't be successful and rich by the world's standards, but you will have the best life capable of having.

—ARTIE SHAW

The shoe that fits one person pinches another;
there is no recipe for living that suits all cases.

—CARL JUNG

How we spend our days is, of course, how we spend our lives.

—ANNIE DILLARD

In three words I can sum up everything I've learned about life:
it goes on.

—ROBERT FROST

Life isn't about finding yourself. Life is about creating yourself.

—GEORGE BERNARD SHAW

We must let go of the life we have planned,
so as to accept the one that is waiting for us.

—JOSEPH CAMPBELL

Life is not a having and a getting, but a being and a becoming.

—MATTHEW ARNOLD

It's not what you gather, but what you scatter
that tells what kind of life you have lived.

—HELEN WALTON

We make a living by what we get.
We make a life by what we give.

—AUTHOR UNKNOWN

Love

Love is universal and exists in many forms, revealing itself in different ways, both verbal and non-verbal. Whether it is the love of parent to child, friend to friend, love between romantic partners, or individual to community—love inspires us to be the best we can. Expressing love is the most genuine, caring thing one person can do for another. As I read through the quotes in this chapter, I've rediscovered ideas for expressing love to the people I cherish in my life. I hope it does the same for you.

For one human being to love another, that is perhaps the most difficult of all our tasks, the ultimate, the last test and proof, the work for which all other work is but preparation.

—RAINER MARIA RILKE

Love is that condition in which the happiness of another person is essential to your own.

—ROBERT A. HEINLEIN

Love is sustained by action, a pattern of devotion in the things we do for each other every day.

—NICHOLAS SPARKS

The transformation of the heart is a wondrous thing, no matter how you land there.

—PATTI SMITH

Person to person, moment to moment, as we love, we change the world.

—SAMAHRIA LYTE KAUFMAN

What greater thing is there for human souls than to feel that they are joined for life— to be with each other in silent unspeakable memories.

—GEORGE ELIOT

You, yourself, as much as anybody in the universe, deserve your love and affection.

—THE BUDDHA

Anyone can be passionate, but it takes real lovers to be silly.

—ROSE FRANKEN

163

Certain things in life simply have to be experienced— and never explained. Love is such a thing.

—PAULO COELHO

It's no trick loving somebody at their best. Love is loving someone at their worst.

—TOM STOPPARD

We can only learn to love by loving.

—IRIS MURDOCH

Every act of love is a work of peace no matter how small.

—Blessed Mother Teresa

Blessed is the influence of one true, loving human soul
on another.

—George Eliot

Love one another, but make not a bond of love: Let it rather
be a moving sea between the shores of your souls.

—Kahlil Gibran

The first duty of love is to listen.

—Paul Tillich

At the end of my life, when I ask one final, "What have I done?"
let my answer be: I have done love.

—Jennifer Pastiloff

You will find as you look back upon your life that the moments
when you have truly lived are the moments when you have done
things in the spirit of love.

—Henry Drummond

Don't look for big things,
just do small things with great love.

—Blessed Mother Teresa

The one thing we can never get enough of us is love.
And the one thing we never give enough of is love.

—Henry Miller

You will learn a lot from yourself if you stretch in the direction
of goodness, of bigness, of kindness, of forgiveness,
of emotional bravery. Be a warrior for love.

—Cheryl Strayed

165

Lovers don't finally meet somewhere.
They're in each other all along.

—Rumi

Love consists of this: two solitudes that meet, protect,
and greet each other.

—Rainer Maria Rilke

At one glance
I loved you with a thousand hearts.

—Mihri Hatun

Love one another as I have loved you,
so you must love one another.

—JOHN 13:34

The most important thing in this world
is to learn to give out love, and let it come in.

—MITCH ALBOM

Love is the first ingredient in the relief of human suffering.

—PADRE PIO

Life has taught us that love does not consist of gazing at each
other, but in looking outward together in the same direction.

—ANTOINE DE SAINT-EXUPÉRY

There is nothing love cannot face;
there is no limit to its faith, its hope, and its endurance.

—ST. PAUL I CORINTHIANS 13:7

Mindfulness

Mindfulness is the practice of slowing down or meditating to bring attention to the present moment. Many of us have frequent thoughts about regretting the past or worrying about the future. Mindfulness is focusing on the moment as it is. It's an excellent way to reduce stress and grow more appreciative of life. Make the choice to slow down, take time, and recalibrate yourself to the present. By doing so, you can reduce stress and anxiety, and learn to appreciate the magnificence of the world around you. The quotes here will spark awareness in yourself and encourage you to reflect on the present moment.

Be here now and savor the delight of the present moment.
—DEEPAK CHOPRA

Wherever you go, there you are.
—JON KABAT-ZINN

168

If you live in awareness, it is easy to see miracles everywhere.
—THÍCH NHẤT HẠNH

This moment is all there is.
—RUMI

Let the breath lead the way.
—SHARON SALZBERG

*You must learn to be still in the midst of activity
and to be vibrantly alive in repose.*

—INDIRA GANDHI

Realize deeply that the present moment is all you ever have.

—ECKHART TOLLE

To the mind that is still, the whole universe surrenders.

—LAO TZU

169

*The secret of health for both mind and body is not to mourn
for the past, worry about the future, or anticipate troubles,
but to live in the present moment wisely and earnestly.*

—THE BUDDHA

When a moment matters, life matters.

—TAL BEN-SHAHAR

The feeling that any task is a nuisance
will soon disappear if it is done in mindfulness.

—THÍCH NHẤT HẠNH

The moment one gives close attention to anything, even a
blade of grass, it becomes a mysterious, awesome, indescribably
magnificent world in itself.

—HENRY MILLER

Soak it in. Don't take a picture. Enjoy it right this second.

—MAYA RUDOLPH

Be mindful even if your mind is full.

—JAMES DE LA VEGA

Rest is not idleness, and to lie sometimes on the grass under
trees on a summer's day, listening to the murmur of the water,
or watching the clouds float across the sky, is by no means a
waste of time.

—JOHN LUBBOCK

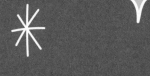

We must slow down to a human tempo and we'll begin
to have time to listen.

—THOMAS MERTON

If we could see the miracle of a single flower,
our whole life would change.

—JACK KORNFIELD

Mindfulness is a choice, and it is something we can practice.
When our mind wanders—whether while eating, doing the dishes,
writing a report, or walking to our car—we can gently shift our
focus back to the wonders that are everywhere to be found.

—TAL BEN-SHAHAR

The miracle is to walk on the green earth
in the present moment, to appreciate
the peace and beauty that are available now.

—THÍCH NHẤT HẠNH

Motherhood

How could I have known in my early twenties that I would adore becoming a mother in my late twenties? As much as I knew that I wanted to become a mother, there was no way of knowing that the process of motherhood would create such unexpected happiness coupled with great exhaustion (in the early years). As a mother, I would do anything to nurture and protect my children. Some of the larger challenges came when I wanted to teach my children the skills they would need to grow into adults. As mothers, we want to raise our children to be the best they can be throughout their lives. I hope some of the thoughts here offer inspiration for life's greatest gift.

Mother love is the fuel that enables a normal human being to do the impossible.

—Marion C. Garretty

Motherhood is the most completely humbling experience I've ever had.

—Diane Keaton

One thing I learned from watching chimpanzees with their infants is that having a child should be fun.

—Jane Goodall

Cleaning your house while your kids are still growing is like shoveling the walk before it stops snowing.

—Phyllis Diller

If mama ain't happy, ain't nobody happy.

—Tracy Byrd

[My mother] had handed down respect for the possibilities—
and the will to grasp them.

—ALICE WALKER

*Being a mother is not about what you gave up to have a child,
but what you've gained from having one.*

—AUTHOR UNKNOWN

We all carry our mothers inside of us.

—KATHERINE CENTER

*I love my mother for all the times she said absolutely nothing....
Thinking back on it all, it must have been the most difficult
part of mothering she ever had to do: knowing the outcome, yet
feeling she had no right to keep me from charting my own path.
I thank her for all her virtues, but mostly for never once having
said, "I told you so."*

—ERMA BOMBECK

If you want your children to turn out well,
spend twice as much time with them, and half as much money.

—ABIGAIL VAN BUREN

It's not our job to toughen our children up to face a cruel and
heartless world. It's our job to raise children who will make
the world a little less cruel and heartless.

—L. R. KNOST

Your children make it impossible to regret your past.
They're its finest fruits.

—ANNA QUINDLEN

There is eternal influence and power in motherhood.

—JULIE B. BACK

Kids learn more from example than anything you say. I'm
convinced they learn very early not to hear anything you say
but watch what you do.

—JANE PAULEY

A child's hand in yours—what tenderness and power it arouses.
You are instantly the very touchstone of wisdom and strength.

—Marjorie Holmes

When in doubt, choose the kids.
There will be plenty of time later to choose the work.

—Anna Quindlen

There's no way to be a perfect mother
and a million ways to be a good one.

—Jill Churchill

Motherhood has taught me the meaning of living in the moment
and being at peace. Children don't think about yesterday, and
they don't think about tomorrow. They just exist in the moment.

—Jessalyn Gilsig

When you are a mother, you are never really alone in your thoughts. A mother always has to think twice, once for herself and once for her child.

—Sophia Loren

The hand that rocks the cradle is the hand that rules the world.

—W. R. Wallace

The mother's heart is the child's schoolroom.

—Henry Ward Beecher

I remember my mother's prayers and they have always followed me. They have clung to me all my life.

—Abraham Lincoln

Be the mom you want them to remember.

—Author unknown

Passion

Passion captures the bliss of new discovery, learning, and finding purpose. When something you discover brings joy, has meaning, hang on to that thing. It can refuel you when you are feeling low, or it can drive you to new pursuits and open new doors. I find the words in this chapter to be invigorating; inspiring me to go after the things that excite me. I hope you discover similar enthusiasm as you read this chapter.

Let yourself be silently drawn by the strange pull
of what you really love.

—RUMI

Nothing is as important as passion.
No matter what you want to do with your life, be passionate.

—JON BON JOVI

Certain things catch your eye,
but pursue only those that capture the heart

—ANCIENT INDIAN PROVERB

Find what brings you joy and go there.

—JAN PHILLIPS

Follow your bliss and the universe will open doors
where there were only walls.

—JOSEPH CAMPBELL

If you have two or three real passions, don't feel like you have
to pick and choose between them. Don't discard.
Keep all your passions in your life.

—AUSTIN KLEON

Doing what you love is the cornerstone of having abundance
in your life.

—WAYNE DYER

The things that excite you are not random.
They are connected to your purpose. Follow them.

—TERRIE DAVOLL HUDSON

To do what you love and feel that it matters;
how could anything be more fun?

—KATHERINE GRAHAM

One of the more powerful outbreaks of happiness and meaning
in your life will occur when you pair your passion
and the world's need.

—SUE MONK KIDD

Don't ask what the world needs. Ask what makes you come alive
and go do it. Because what the world needs is people
who have come alive.

—HOWARD THURMAN

You cannot give your life more days,
but you can give your days more life.

—AUTHOR UNKNOWN

Be in love with your life. Every detail of it.

—JACK KEROUAC

Peace

Peace is not a passive noun. It is a continuous, active practice that must be continually reaffirmed each day. Peace begins with the individual. We must realize that we are not powerless and that the power of one can make a difference. An important step for finding peace in the entire world is finding peace within ourselves. I cherish the opportunity to reflect on the wisdom in this chapter. By working on what we can control, our individual peace; our hope is to join efforts with others to create world peace among all people and nations.

Peace is every step.

—THÍCH NHẤT HẠNH

Let us, on both sides, lay aside all arrogance. Let us not, on either side, claim that we have already discovered the truth.

—ST. AUGUSTINE

When you find peace within yourself, you become the kind of person who can live at peace with others.

—PEACE PILGRIM

Peace cannot be kept by force; it can only be achieved by understanding.

—ALBERT EINSTEIN

Peace in its most fundamental form is the connection of one human spirit to another.

—ARCHBISHOP DESMOND TUTU

It isn't enough to talk about peace. One must believe in it.
And it isn't enough to believe in it. One must work at it.

—ELEANOR ROOSEVELT

If you wish to be brothers, drop your weapons.

—POPE JOHN PAUL II

We must seek, above all, a world of peace; a world in which
peoples dwell together in mutual respect and work together
in mutual regard.

—JOHN F. KENNEDY

We can never obtain peace in the outer world
until we make peace within ourselves.

—H. H. DALAI LAMA

It should never be forgotten that peace resides ultimately not in the hands of government, but in the hands of the people.

—HUSSEIN I

An eye for an eye makes the whole world blind.

—MAHATMA GANDHI

I destroy my enemies when I make them my friends.

—ABRAHAM LINCOLN

If you want peace, work for justice.

—POPE PAUL VI

Peace comes when our hearts are open like the sky, vast as the ocean.

—JACK KORNFIELD

Perseverance

Through perseverance and tenacity, we discover who we can become. Perseverance is our steadfast effort to do or achieve something despite difficulties and obstacles. While a particular goal may seem unlikely or impossible, each step we take brings us closer to success. Perseverance is an important character trait to develop early in life, but it is also a welcome attribute to develop at any age. Throughout it all, perseverance proves the impossible is attainable.

We are made to persist. That's how we find out who we are.

—Tobias Wolff

I will persist until I succeed... Always will I take another step.
If that is of no avail, I will take another, and yet another. In
truth, one step at a time is not too difficult.... I know that
small attempts, repeated, will complete any undertaking.

—Og Mandino

You never know how strong you are until being strong
is the only choice you have.

—Bob Marley

It always seems impossible until it's done.

—Nelson Mandela

My philosophy is that not only are you responsible for your life,
but doing the best at this moment puts you in the best place
for the next moment.

—Oprah Winfrey

Work hard. Do good. Be incredible.

—Cheryl Strayed

*At the end of the day,
we can endure much more than we think we can.*

—FRIDA KAHLO

*We must have perseverance and above all confidence in
ourselves. We must believe that we are gifted for something
and that this thing must be attained.*

—MARIE CURIE

Never confuse a single defeat with a final defeat.

—F. SCOTT FITZGERALD

*We all get stuck in place on occasion. We all move backward
sometimes. Every day we must make the decision to move in
the direction of our intentions.
Forward is the direction of real life.*

—CHERYL STRAYED

There is something inside you that is greater than any obstacle.

—CHRISTIAN D. LARSON

*Get a good idea and stay with it.
Do it, and work at it until it's done.*

—WALT DISNEY

Make the most of yourself by fanning the tiny, inner sparks of possibility into flames of achievement.

—GOLDA MEIR

I am not discouraged, because every wrong attempt discarded is another step forward.

—THOMAS EDISON

If I have the belief that I can do it, I shall surely acquire the capacity to do it even if I may not have it at the beginning.

—MAHATMA GANDHI

With each new day comes new strength and new thoughts.

—ELEANOR ROOSEVELT

When you have exhausted all possibilities, remember this: You haven't.

—THOMAS EDISON

Perspective

The great thing about perspective is that there's always more than one. For any situation in which we find ourselves, if we take one step to the left or one step to the right, or if we look up, down, or all around, we might discover something different. I've always considered our frame of mind to be something we can choose to change because every day we may be faced with challenges that can be overcome by a shift in viewpoint. I've included quotes in this chapter that will offer some welcome ideas for improving your perspective.

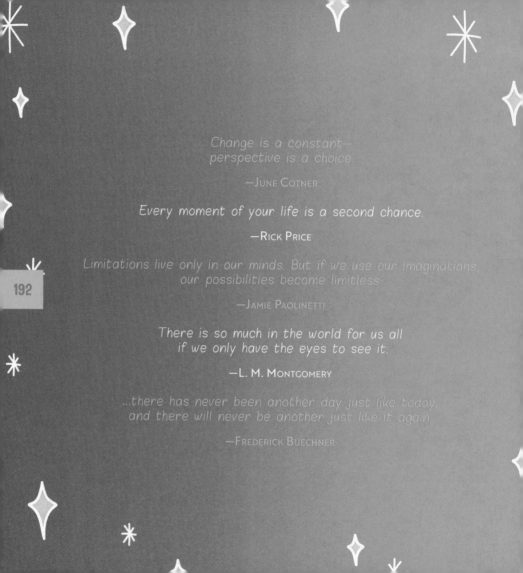

Change is a constant—
perspective is a choice.

—JUNE COTNER

Every moment of your life is a second chance.

—RICK PRICE

Limitations live only in our minds. But if we use our imaginations,
our possibilities become limitless.

—JAMIE PAOLINETTI

There is so much in the world for us all
if we only have the eyes to see it.

—L. M. MONTGOMERY

...there has never been another day just like today,
and there will never be another just like it again.

—FREDERICK BUECHNER

*We have no idea what tomorrow will bring,
but today is overflowing with potential.*

—ALLAN LOKOS

*When there's a big disappointment, we don't know if that's
the end of the story. It may just be the beginning of a
great adventure.*

—PEMA CHÖDRÖN

*If we all threw our problems in a pile
and saw everyone else's, we'd grab ours back.*

—REGINA BRETT

*When you arise in the morning, think of what a privilege it is to
be alive, to think, to enjoy, to love.*

—MARCUS AURELIUS

*Worry does not empty tomorrow of its sorrow,
it empties today of its strength.*

—CORRIE TEN BOOM

The world is so constructed, that if you wish to enjoy its pleasures, you must also endure its pains. Whether you like it or not, you cannot have one without the other.

—SWAMI BRAHMANANDA

No longer forward or behind I look in hope or fear;
But, grateful, take the good I find, The best of now and here.

—JOHN GREENLEAF WHITTIER

Human beings must always be on the watch for the coming of wonders.

—E. B. WHITE

We will find what we look for. When we look for humor, beauty, or joy, we will discover them all around us.

—MARY PIPHER

Each day, each of us is faced with the possibility of resetting our lives. Refocusing. Reimagining. Rebooting. Every day, we can decide to change our outlook, our words, our tone, and our attitude.

—MARIA SHRIVER

Although no one can go back and make a brand-new start, anyone can start from now and make a brand-new ending.

—CARL BARD

You don't have a right to the cards you believe you should have been dealt. You have an obligation to play the hell out of the ones you're holding.

—CHERYL STRAYED

Little by little, one walks far.

—PERUVIAN PROVERB

195

This is not how your story ends. It's simply where it takes a turn you didn't expect.

—CHERYL STRAYED

I want to stay as close to the edge as I can without going over. Out on the edge you see all kinds of things you can't see from the center.

—KURT VONNEGUT

No pessimist ever discovered the secret of the stars, or sailed an uncharted land, or opened a new doorway for the human spirit.

—HELEN KELLER

This is a wonderful day. I've never seen this one before.

—MAYA ANGELOU

I am an old man and have known a great many troubles, but most of them never happened.

—MARK TWAIN

If you change the way you look at things, the things you look at change.

—WAYNE DYER

It is better to have faith in everybody and be deceived occasionally than to mistrust everybody and be deceived almost constantly.

—CHRISTIAN D. LARSON

Sometimes I go about pitying myself, when all the while I am being carried by great winds across the sky.

—OJIBWA SAYING

What you see and hear depends a good deal on where you are standing; it also depends on what kind of person you are.

—C. S. Lewis

Think big thoughts but relish small pleasures.

—H. Jackson Brown Jr.

And in the end, it's not the years in your life that count. It's the life in your years.

—Edward J. Stieglitz

We don't see things as they are, we see them as we are.

—Anaïs Nin

It isn't the great pleasures that count the most; it's making a great deal out of the little ones.

—Jean Webster

What we see depends mainly on what we look for.

—John Lubbock

You can become blind by seeing each day as a similar one. Each day is a different one, each day brings a miracle of its own. It's just a matter of paying attention to this miracle.

—PAULO COELHO

You are braver than you believe, stronger than you seem, and smarter than you think.

—A. A. MILNE

You can never step into the same river twice; for new waters are always flowing on to you.

—HERACLITUS

For everything you have missed, you have gained something else.

—RALPH WALDO EMERSON

Barn's burnt down—now I can see the moon.

—MIZUTA MASAHIDE

Don't wait. The time will never be just right.

—NAPOLEON HILL

Pets

Having a pet is like having a secret window into the world of unconditional love and joy. Pets adore us and they don't judge us; they are part of our everyday lives and part of our families. Besides companionship, they reduce stress levels and loneliness, and they increase our physical and social activities. An added health benefit is that people with pets typically have lower heart rates, lower cholesterol, and lower blood pressure. Pets also can add immensely to a child's comfort and self-esteem. Often humorous in their truthfulness, the words in this chapter remind us to appreciate the simplicity and positivity of the creatures we are fortunate enough to have in our lives.

An animal's eyes have the power to speak a great language.

—MARTIN BUBER

I believe all creatures are God's masterpieces, but I also think most members of the human race could use some spiritual touching up by the artist. Dogs definitely play a part as spiritual messengers to help with that touch-up. Dogs are healers. They are enlightened. They seem to have figured out how to live beautifully so much better than we humans have. While we struggle to figure out why we were put here on Earth, all a dog wants is to love and be loved—a powerful lesson for us all.

—BERNIE SIEGEL

Scratch a dog and you'll find a permanent job.

—FRANKLIN P. JONES

Sometimes you don't need words to feel better; you just need the nearness of your dog.

—NATALIE LLOYD

My goal in life is to be as good of a person my dog already thinks I am.

—AUTHOR UNKNOWN

THE DIFFERENCE BETWEEN DOGS AND CATS

A dog thinks: Hey, these people I live with feed me, love me, provide me with a nice warm, dry house, pet me, and take good care of me... They must be gods!

A cat thinks: Hey, these people I live with feed me, love me, provide me with a nice warm, dry house, pet me, and take good care of me... I must be a god!

—AUTHOR UNKNOWN

When I play with my cat, who knows if I am not a pastime to her more than she is to me?

—MONTAIGNE

Is there anything more satisfying on a cold, blustery day, than a good book, a hearty fire, and a soft purring friend by your side?

—MARY MAUDE DANIELS

CATS AS TEACHERS

*We have learned many things from living with [our cats].
Some lessons are directives we would be wise to follow: Live
a rhythmic life. Sit and savor the present moment. Gaze
intently. Stretch often. Keep out of harm's way. Take good care
of your family. Be independent, but don't be afraid of being
dependent on others. Cherish your wildness, even if no one else
does. When you want something, be persistent. When someone
pays attention to you, respond with affection. If you are
embarrassed, turn your back on the situation and get on with
your life. Enjoy small treats. Keep yourself clean. Take a nap
when you need one, and try to relax more.*

—FREDERIC AND MARY ANN BRUSSAT

*The essential joy of being with horses is that it brings us
in contact with the rare elements of grace, beauty, spirit,
and freedom.*

—SHARON RALLS LEMON

*If having a soul means being able to feel love and loyalty and
gratitude, then animals are better off than a lot of humans.*

—JAMES HERRIOT

In their innocence and wisdom, in their connection to the earth and its most ancient rhythms, animals show us a way back to a home they have never left.

—SUSAN CHERNAK MCELROY

Animals are such agreeable friends— they ask no questions, they pass no criticisms...

—GEORGE ELIOT

I have found that when you are deeply troubled there are things you get from the silent devoted companionship of a dog that you can get from no other source.

—DORIS DAY

The greatness of a nation and its moral progress can be judged by the way its animals are treated.

—MAHATMA GANDHI

By ethical conduct toward all creatures, we enter into a spiritual relationship with the universe.

—ALBERT SCHWEITZER

Positivity

Optimism, possibility, laughter, and joy. These are the elements of positivity that keep us moving forward through challenges and change. The infectiousness of a positive attitude can make an enormous difference in how we see the world. Brain scientists have discovered that when people are asked to imagine an optimistic future, more areas of the brain light up during MRIs than when people focus on a negative or neutral future. Our brains work better when we think positively. We are more creative, happy, tolerant, successful, solution-oriented, and good-natured.

Optimism is the faith that leads to achievement. Nothing can be done without hope and confidence.

—HELEN KELLER

I'm hoping to be astonished tomorrow by I don't know what.

—JIM HARRISON

To be alive, to be able to see, to walk...it's all a miracle. I have adapted the technique of living life from miracle to miracle.

—ARTHUR RUBINSTEIN

Become a possibilitarian. No matter how dark things seem to be or actually are, raise your sights and see possibilities— always see them, for they're always there.

—NORMAN VINCENT PEALE

Every day we should hear at least one little song, read one good poem, see one exquisite picture, and, if possible, speak a few sensible words.

—JOHANN WOLFGANG VON GOETHE

Write it on your heart that every day is the best day in the year.

—RALPH WALDO EMERSON

Change your thoughts and you change your world.

—NORMAN VINCENT PEALE

The most wasted of all days is one without laughter.

—NICOLAS CHAMFORT

Every time you replace a fearful thought with a loving thought,
you make the world a better place.

—DENISE LINN

The thoughts we choose to think are the tools
we use to paint the canvas of our lives.

—LOUISE L. HAY

The best thing about the future
is that it comes one day at a time.

—ABRAHAM LINCOLN

Somewhere, something incredible is waiting to be known.

—CARL SAGAN

You are always on your way to a miracle.

—SARK

Purpose

What is purpose? It is an objective or goal through which we can achieve fulfillment and success. It is the reason we get up in the morning and stay motivated throughout the day. Purpose gives life meaning. It can guide important decisions, influence behavior, shape goals, and offer a sense of direction. This chapter will help you recognize your unique gifts and how you can use them to contribute to the world.

> Doubt everything. Find your own light.
>
> —THE BUDDHA

> The equation for purpose is G + P + V = P.
> (Gifts + Passions + Values = Purpose)
>
> —RICHARD LEIDER

> The meaning of life is to find your gift.
> The purpose of life is to give it away.
>
> —PABLO PICASSO

> Forget past mistakes. Forget failures. Forget everything except
> what you're going to do now and do it.
>
> —WILL DURANT

> The most fulfilled people are those who get up every morning
> and stand for something larger than themselves.
>
> —WILMA MANKILLER

> You cannot go through a single day without having an impact on
> the world around you. What you do makes a difference, and you
> have to decide what kind of difference you want to make.
>
> —JANE GOODALL

Nothing contributes so much to tranquilize the mind
as a steady purpose.

—MARY SHELLEY

Light tomorrow with today.

—ELIZABETH BARRETT BROWNING

If you ask me what I came into this life to do,
I will tell you: I came to live out loud.

—ÉMILE ZOLA

This is the true joy in life—
being used for a purpose recognized by yourself
as a mighty one.

—GEORGE BERNARD SHAW

211

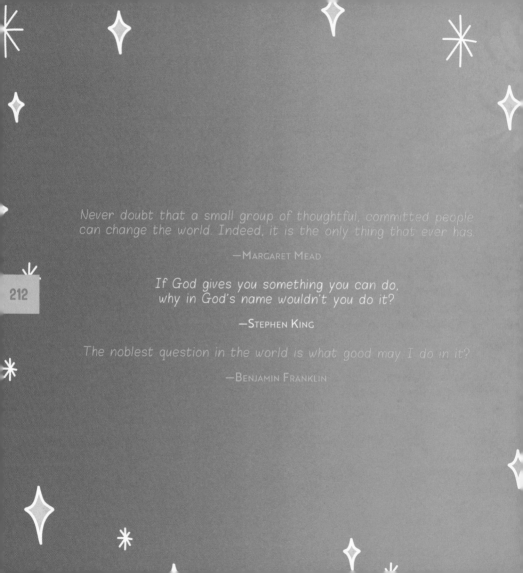

Never doubt that a small group of thoughtful, committed people can change the world. Indeed, it is the only thing that ever has.

—MARGARET MEAD

If God gives you something you can do, why in God's name wouldn't you do it?

—STEPHEN KING

The noblest question in the world is what good may I do in it?

—BENJAMIN FRANKLIN

Reflections

The gift of reflection is something I take very seriously. Every quote in this chapter can be reconsidered, allowing ourselves the time to mull it over and decide how it resonates with each of us. How often does a moment of reflection within our busy lives allow us a renewed opportunity to see something from a new perspective or come to a realization we wouldn't otherwise have had? I encourage you to take your time with this chapter, and enjoy what inspiration comes from your own reflections.

You are strong when you know your weaknesses. You are beautiful when you appreciate your flaws. You are wise when you learn from your mistakes.

—AUTHOR UNKNOWN

All endings are also beginnings, we just don't know it at the time.

—MITCH ALBOM

214

I think, what has this day brought me, and what have I given it?

—HENRY MOORE

Coincidence is God's way of remaining anonymous.

—AUTHOR UNKNOWN

Like a sandcastle, all is temporary. Build it, tend it, enjoy it. And when the time comes, let it go.

—JACK KORNFIELD

Life is a balance between holding on and letting go.

—RUMI

*Sometimes your limitations can be a launching pad
into an unexpected story.*

—DANA TANAMACHI

*Let's not look back in anger, or forward in fear,
but around in awareness.*

—JAMES THURBER

*The best and most beautiful things in this world
cannot be seen or even touched,
but must be felt with the heart.*

—HELEN KELLER

215

I am so absorbed in the wonder of earth and the life upon it
that I cannot think of heaven and the angels.
I have enough for this life.

—PEARL S. BUCK

*If only you could sense how important you are to the lives of
those you meet; how important you can be to people you may
never even dream of. There is something of yourself that you
leave at every meeting with another person.*

—FRED ROGERS

People often say that "beauty is in the eye of the beholder,"
and I say that the most liberating thing about beauty
is realizing that you are the beholder.
This empowers us to find beauty in places where others have
not dared to look, including inside ourselves.

—SALMA HAYEK

How silent the woods would be if only the best birds sang.

—REVEREND DALE TURNER

Today you will witness countless miracles,
starting with the sun's dawning.

—CORRINE DE WINTER

You can tell what your values are
by looking at how you spend your extra money.

—GLORIA STEINEM

*Not everything that can be counted counts,
and not everything that counts can be counted.*

—William Bruce Cameron

*How far you go in life depends on your being tender with the
young, compassionate with the aged, sympathetic with the
striving, and tolerant of the weak and strong. Because someday
in life you will have been all of these.*

—George Washington Carver

*When we do the best we can, we never know what miracle is
wrought in our life, or in the life of another.*

—Helen Keller

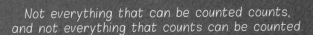

What would you do if you weren't afraid?

—Spencer Johnson

The best way out is always through.

—Robert Frost

Time is the coin of your life. You spend it.
Do not allow others to spend it for you.

—Carl Sandburg

We all take different paths in life, but no matter where we go,
we take a little of each other everywhere.

—Tim McGraw

218

We spend so much time being afraid of failure, afraid of
rejection. But regret is the thing we should fear most.

—Trevor Noah

What we do in life echoes in Eternity.

—Maximus in *Gladiator*

Beautiful young people are accidents of nature,
but beautiful old people are works of art.

—Eleanor Roosevelt

Cherish all your happy moments:
They make a fine cushion for old age.

—BOOTH TARKINGTON

We are not independent but interdependent.

—THE BUDDHA

If you realized how powerful your thoughts are,
you would never think a negative thought.

—PEACE PILGRIM

We shall not cease from exploration
And the end of all our exploring
Will be to arrive where we started
And know the place for the first time.

—T. S. ELIOT

It is so small a thing to have enjoyed the sun, to have lived
light in the spring, to have loved, to have thought, to have done.

—MATTHEW ARNOLD

What lies behind us and what lies before us
are tiny matters compared to what lies within us.

—RALPH WALDO EMERSON

Renewal

Renewal, a time to take a break and practice self-care, is a vital part of our holistic health. For some, seeking that renewal means solitude, peace, silence, or nature. For others, it could mean creating or enjoying art, getting together with friends, or practicing service. Whatever the method, this chapter offers inspiration for rejuvenation—in strength, in joy, in creativity, and in purpose.

Rest when you're weary.
Refresh and renew yourself, your body, your mind, your spirit.

—RALPH MARSTON

The best remedy for those who are afraid, lonely or unhappy is
to go outside, somewhere where they can be quiet, alone with
the heavens, nature, and God.

—ANNE FRANK

If you can spend a perfectly useless afternoon in a perfectly
useless manner, you have learned how to live.

—LIN YUTANG

Happiness is the art of relaxation.

—MAXWELL MALTZ

Let the rain sing you a lullaby.

—LANGSTON HUGHES

I never found the companion that was so companionable
as solitude.

—HENRY DAVID THOREAU

*If you empty yourself of yesterday's sorrows,
you will have much more room for today's joy.*

—JENNI YOUNG

Sometimes you need to take a break from everyone and spend
time alone, to experience, appreciate, and love yourself.

—ROBERT TEW

223

*Allow yourself to rest. Your soul speaks to you
in the quiet moments in between your thoughts.*

—AUTHOR UNKNOWN

Everybody needs beauty as well as bread, places to play in and
pray in, where nature may heal and cheer and give strength to
body and soul alike.

—JOHN MUIR

The final stage of healing is using what happens to you to help other people. That is healing in itself.

—GLORIA STEINEM

Learn to get in touch with the silence within yourself and know that everything in this life has a purpose.

—ELISABETH KÜBLER-ROSS

There must be quite a few things that a hot bath won't cure, but I don't know any of them.

—SYLVIA PLATH

One way to open your eyes is to ask yourself, "What if I had never seen this before? What if I knew I would never see it again?"

—RACHEL CARSON

Every day is a new opportunity to change your life. You have the power to say, "This is not how my story ends."

—KAREN SALMANSOHN

Be gentle with yourself. You are a child of the universe, no less than the trees and the stars. In the noisy confusion of life, keep peace in your soul.

—Max Ehrmann

We've known about the transcendent power of solitude for centuries; it's only recently that we've forgotten it.

—Susan Cain

There is no need to go to India or anywhere else to find peace. You will find that deep place of silence right in your room, your garden, or even your bathtub.

—Elisabeth Kübler-Ross

No one likes crying, but tears water our souls.

—Xue Xinran

I only went out for a walk, and finally concluded to stay out till sundown, for going out, I found I was really going in.

—JOHN MUIR

Listening to the birds can be a meditation
if you listen with awareness.

—OSHO

Together with a culture of work, there must be a culture of leisure as gratification. To put it another way: people who work must take the time to relax, to be with their families, to enjoy themselves, read, listen to music, play a sport.

—POPE FRANCIS

There must be always remaining in every life, some place for the singing of angels, some place for that which in itself is breathless and beautiful.

—HOWARD THURMAN

Serenity

Serenity is defined as the state of being calm and peaceful. Many circumstances in modern life affect our sense of peace and contentment—stressful jobs, relationship difficulties, day-to-day worries, and a sense of feeling overwhelmed with the hyperspeed demands of life. Serenity is not the lack of conflict or strife, but an acceptance of the moment, a concentration inward to still our own spirit, and the stability of not needing to always be moving. The quotes here offer helpful thoughts, perspectives, and insights that encourage us to create more peace, joy, and tranquility in our lives.

*Within you there is a stillness and a sanctuary
to which you can retreat at any time and be yourself.*

—HERMAN HESSE

The earth has its music for those who listen.

—REGINALD VINCENT HOLMES

Quiet the mind enough so it is the heart that gives the prayer.

—INGRID GOFF-MAIDOFF

Be content with what you have; rejoice in the way things are.
When you realize there is nothing lacking,
the whole world belongs to you.

—LAO TZU

*When the mind looks outward, it is swayed by the heavy winds
of the world. But when the mind faces inward, we can find
our center and rest in stillness.*

—HAEMIN SUNIM

Serenity is not freedom from the storm,
but peace amid the storm.

—AUTHOR UNKNOWN

When you connect to the silence within you, that is when you can make sense of the disturbance going on around you.

—STEPHEN RICHARDS

Stepping out of the busyness, stopping our endless pursuit of getting somewhere else, is perhaps the most beautiful offering we can make to our spirit.

—TARA BRACH

Rivers know this:
There is no hurry.
We shall get there some day.

—A. A. MILNE

THE SERENITY PRAYER

God grant me the serenity to accept
the things I cannot change,
courage to change the things I can,
and wisdom to know the difference.

—REINHOLD NIEBUHR

Service

It is sometimes through acts of service that we learn how strong we are. Every person's contribution may be different, whether it's serving in a soup kitchen, tutoring a student, picking up litter, or acting as a street medic during a protest. The quotes here inspire us with their acknowledgement of the value of small acts, the exhilaration that comes with doing good, and the joy that comes with making a difference. What service are you inspired to perform today?

How wonderful it is that nobody need wait a single moment
before starting to improve the world.

—ANNE FRANK

Hands that serve are holier than lips that pray.

—SAI BABA

If you light a lamp for someone else it will also brighten
your path.

—THE BUDDHA

Whatever your cause, have fun along the way.

—JUNE COTNER

Life's most persistent and urgent question is,
"What are you doing for others?"

—DR. MARTIN LUTHER KING JR.

Attention is the rarest and purest form of generosity.

—SIMONE WEIL

Service is the rent you pay for being.

—MARIAN WRIGHT EDELMAN

I've been put on the planet to serve humanity.
I have to remind myself to live simply and not to overindulge,
which is a constant battle in a material world.

—SANDRA CISNEROS

I am a little pencil in the hand of a writing God
who is sending a love letter to the world.

—BLESSED MOTHER TERESA

Do your little bit of good where you are; it's those little bits
of good put together that overwhelm the world.

—ARCHBISHOP DESMOND TUTU

233

Small acts, when multiplied by millions of people,
can transform the world.

—HOWARD ZINN

I slept and dreamt that life was joy. I awoke and saw
that life was service. I acted and behold, service was joy.

—DR. MARTIN LUTHER KING JR.

We are all like one-winged angels.
It's only when we help each other that we can fly.

—LUCIANO DE CRESCENZO

Use every letter you write, every conversation you have, every meeting you attend, to express your fundamental beliefs and dreams. Affirm to others the vision of the world you want. You are a free, immensely powerful source of life and goodness. Affirm it. Spread it. Radiate it. Think day and night about it and you will see a miracle happen: the greatness of your own life.

—ROBERT MULLER

To do something, however small, to make others happier and better, is the highest ambition, the most elevating hope, which can inspire a human being.

—JOHN LUBBOCK

It is one of the beautiful compensations in this life that no one can sincerely try to help another without helping himself.

—RALPH WALDO EMERSON

The best way to find yourself is to lose yourself in the service of others.

—MAHATMA GANDHI

Simplicity

I think frequently about the value of simplicity. The quotes in this chapter remind me how such small moments of present mindfulness can help provide tranquility. When things become complicated, it's usually through slowing down and taking a step back that I appreciate the clarity that is revealed. Contentedness seems to be a major benefit for those who adhere to a simpler lifestyle. Contemplating the words in this chapter reminds me that I have the ability to remove the unnecessary, seek the ordinary, and revel in its wonder. I hope this chapter provides that calming perspective for you, too.

It's the simple things in life that are the most extraordinary.

—PAULO COELHO

In the dew of little things
the heart finds its morning and is refreshed.

—KAHLIL GIBRAN

A leaf fluttered in through the window this morning, as if
supported by the rays of the sun, a bird settled on the fire
escape, joy in the task of coffee, joy accompanied me as
I walked.

—ANAÏS NIN

Collect moments. Not things.

—AUTHOR UNKNOWN

The less you want, the richer you are.

—YANNI

To find the universal elements enough; to find the air and the water exhilarating; to be refreshed by a morning walk or an evening saunter...to be thrilled by the stars at night; to be elated over a bird's nest, or over a wildflower in spring—these are some of the rewards of the simple life.

—John Burroughs

To live content with small means; to seek elegance rather than luxury, and refinement rather than fashion...in a word, to let the spiritual, unbidden and unconscious, grow up through the common. This is to be my symphony.

—William Henry Channing

How many times have you noticed that it's the quiet little moments in the midst of life that seem to give the rest extra-special meaning?

—Fred Rogers

It was so simple. So average...how could he find perfection in such an ordinary day... I realized this was the whole point.

—MITCH ALBOM

It is the sweet, simple things of life
which are the real ones after all.

—LAURA INGALLS WILDER

Simplicity, simplicity, simplicity! I say let your affairs be as two
or three, and not a hundred or a thousand; instead of a million
count half a dozen.

—HENRY DAVID THOREAU

Social Justice

We are in a time of reckoning right now. It is our duty to acknowledge past mistakes and misdeeds and rectify the inequities that have perpetuated for centuries. Marginalized people have known this for their entire lives. There is an opportunity now to become a part of the movement that includes speaking out against social injustice, to discover that we may have innate biases, and to re-train our minds to reject the status quo. The quotes below can help the process. Here are some questions to ask yourself: What can I do differently? What can I learn? How can I help? How can I change?

There is no social-change fairy.
There is only change made by the hands of individuals.

—WINONA LADUKE

There is no "them and us." There is only us.

—GREG BOYLE

Whatever affects one directly, affects all indirectly.

—DR. MARTIN LUTHER KING, JR.

Faith is not enough. We must act on our faith. Inner healing is not enough. We must heal our world. Spiritual practice is not enough. We must have the spiritual courage to stand up against injustice.

—RIANE EISLER

By acting compassionately, by helping to restore justice and to encourage peace, we are acknowledging that we are all part of one another.

—RAM DASS

I'm really interested in social justice, and if an artist has a certain power of being heard and voicing something important, it's right to do it. It could still be done in such a way that it's not aggressive or overly didactic. I'm trying to find that form.

—Shirin Neshat

In a racist society it is not enough to be non-racist, we must be anti-racist.

—Angela Davis

Injustice anywhere is a threat to justice everywhere.

—Dr. Martin Luther King Jr.

It is not enough to be compassionate— you must act.

—H. H. Dalai Lama

True peace required the presence of justice, not just the absence of conflict.

—N.K. Jemisin

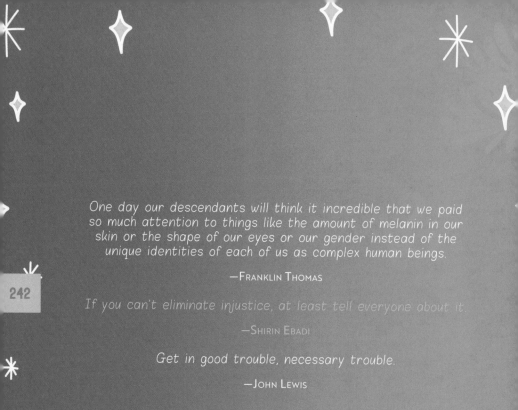

One day our descendants will think it incredible that we paid so much attention to things like the amount of melanin in our skin or the shape of our eyes or our gender instead of the unique identities of each of us as complex human beings.

—FRANKLIN THOMAS

242

If you can't eliminate injustice, at least tell everyone about it.

—SHIRIN EBADI

Get in good trouble, necessary trouble.

—JOHN LEWIS

Spirituality

We often hear the phrase "spiritual, but not religious." Though all religions emphasize spiritualism, one can embrace the spiritual without following specific religious beliefs. The sacred is something that most of us strive to achieve within ourselves. It is the recognition that every living thing in the world is connected to every other living thing, and we yearn to feel that connection. Perhaps it is the mystery of the spiritual that perpetuates our wonder at the world.

There is a voice that doesn't use words. Listen.

—RUMI

Put your ear down close to your soul and listen hard.

—ANNE SEXTON

244

At any moment, you have a choice,
that either leads you closer to your spirit
or further away from it.

—THÍCH NHẤT HẠNH

There is an hour in the darkest of night
when I know you are listening.

—NANCY TUPPER LING

Who looks outside, dreams. Who looks inside, awakens.

—CARL JUNG

The most beautiful experience we can have is the mysterious—the fundamental emotion which stands at the cradle of true art and true science.

—Albert Einstein

The sacred is not in heaven or far away. It is all around us, and small human rituals can connect us to its presence.

—Alma Luz Villanueva

The spiritual life does not remove us from the world but leads us deeper into it.

—Henri J. M. Nouwen

245

We are not human beings having a spiritual experience. We are spiritual beings having a human experience.

—Pierre Teilhard de Chardin

What you seek is seeking you.

—Rumi

Success

The ultimate success is living life in your own way. It is entirely unique to each individual. Often, people start with smaller goals that they feel confident they can achieve and then they keep building from there. Individuals develop many skills along the way. You will feel most satisfied if you pursue goals that you are passionate about and that are consistent with your values. Achieving success can also change over the course of a lifetime. Success in my twenties was nothing like the success of my thirties or forties. For every success, we must acknowledge the obstacles and celebrate the challenges we have overcome to arrive at that moment.

Success is to be measured not so much by the position that one has reached in life as by the obstacles which he has overcome while trying to succeed.

—Booker T. Washington

To laugh often and much, to win the respect of intelligent people and the affection of children; to earn the appreciation of honest critics and endure the betrayal of false friends; to appreciate beauty; to find the best in others; to leave the world a bit better, whether by a healthy child, a garden patch, or a redeemed social condition; to know even one life has breathed easier because you have lived.
This is to have succeeded.

—Ralph Waldo Emerson

It's never too late to be what you might have been.

—George Eliot

When I found I had crossed that line, I looked at my hands to see if I was the same person. There was such a glory over everything; the sun came like gold through the trees, and over the fields, and I felt like I was in heaven.

—Harriet Tubman

There is only one success— to be able
to spend your life in your own way.

—Christopher Darlington Morley

I only went out for a walk, and finally concluded to stay out
till sundown, for going out, I found I was really going in.

—John Muir

Memories of our lives, of our works, and of our deeds
will continue in others.

—Rosa Parks

Success is the sum of small efforts,
repeated day in and day out.

—Robert Collier

We are what we repeatedly do.
Excellence is therefore not an act but a habit.

—Aristotle

Fortune favors the bold.

—Virgil

Travel

Travel, inherently, widens our world perspective. Whether it's visiting family in another state or traveling around the world, there is the opportunity to learn. The journey itself, some would say, is even more important than one's destination. How glorious it is to encounter new cultures, interact with new acquaintances, and find ourselves in the midst of becoming lost.

Once a year, go somewhere you have never been before.

—H. H. Dalai Lama

*Nothing behind me, everything ahead of me,
as is ever so on the road.*

—Jack Kerouac

*A good traveler has no fixed plans
and is not intent upon arriving.*

—Lao Tzu

252

Getting lost is sometimes the best way to find yourself.

—Maxime Lagacé

Travel and change of place impart new vigor to the mind.

—Seneca

Who lives sees, but who travels sees more.

—Ibn Battuta

Not all those who wander are lost.

—J. R. R. Tolkien

Though we travel the world over to find the beautiful,
we must carry it with us or we find it not.

—RALPH WALDO EMERSON

The journey is the destination.

—DAN ELDON

Travel ennobles the spirit and does away with our prejudices.

—OSCAR WILDE

253

I long, as does every human being,
to be at home wherever I find myself.

—MAYA ANGELOU

I travel not to go anywhere, but to go.
I travel for travel's sake.
The great affair is to move.

—ROBERT LOUIS STEVENSON

Wisdom

Wisdom is the ability to think and act using knowledge, experience, understanding, common sense, and insight. The quotes here allow us a moment to reflect on the value of stopping and thinking about certain periods in life—what did this teach me? why is this useful? how is this different? does this bring me peace? Wisdom builds on wisdom; the more we take the time to listen and consider the wisdom we hear, the more we gain in experience and insight—and the wiser we become.

*The person who says it cannot be done
should not interrupt the person who is doing it.*

—CHINESE PROVERB

*Absorb what is useful, discard what is useless,
and add what is specifically your own.*

—BRUCE LEE

What wisdom can you find that is greater than kindness?

—JEAN JACQUES ROUSSEAU

*I have noticed even people who claim everything is predestined,
and that we can do nothing to change it, look before they
cross the road.*

—STEPHEN HAWKING

We learn from difference, not from sameness.

—GLORIA STEINEM

To know how to grow old is the master work of wisdom.

—HENRI FREDERIC AMIEL

What we call wisdom is the result
of all the wisdom of the past ages.

—HENRY WARD BEECHER

You can't unring a bell.

—AUTHOR UNKNOWN

The most unwelcome advice in the world
is that which is unasked for.

—JEANNE PHILLIPS

If you want to be sad, live in the past.
If you want to be anxious, live in the future.
If you want to be peaceful, live in the NOW.

—KAREN SALMANSOHN

Each situation—nay, each moment—is of infinite worth;
for each represents a whole eternity.

—JOHANN WOLFGANG VON GOETHE

Fear less, hope more; eat less, chew more; whine less, breathe
more; talk less, say more; hate less, love more;
and all good things are yours.

—SWEDISH PROVERB

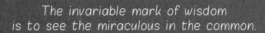

*The invariable mark of wisdom
is to see the miraculous in the common.*

—RALPH WALDO EMERSON

*Love wisdom, and she will guard you; cherish her, and she will
lift you high; if only you embrace her, she will bring you honor.
She will set a garland of grace on your head and bestow on
you a crown of glory.*

—PROVERBS 4:6-9

Wisdom begins in wonder.

—SOCRATES

Affirmations for Living

This chapter was previously titled, "Simple Reminders." My intent was to include short reminders that one could use at any time in life. As I read each quote below, I realized that they qualified as affirmations because they are positive statements that motivate, inspire, and encourage us to take desired action. These quotes can help strengthen our resolve, encourage us toward a decision, ground us in mindfulness, or remind us to be thankful for the moment we have right now. By repeating affirmations, the mental images will influence our behavior, habits, and actions in profound ways.

Instructions for living a life:
Pay attention. Be astonished. Tell about it.

—MARY OLIVER

Look for the best, prepare for the worst, and take what comes.

—AUTHOR UNKNOWN

Be like the hummingbird:
Gather sweetness in all you do.

—JUNE COTNER

The greatest gift we can make to others is our true presence.

—THÍCH NHẤT HẠNH

Start where you are. Use what you have. Do what you can.

—ARTHUR ASHE

What you think, you become. What you feel, you attract.
What you imagine, you create.

—THE BUDDHA

Be mindful. Be grateful. Be positive. Be true. Be kind.

—ROY T. BENNETT

Every moment is a fresh beginning.

—T. S. ELIOT

Be with those who help your being.

—RUMI

*Treasure this day, and treasure yourself.
Truly, neither will ever happen again.*

—RAY BRADBURY

The impossible can always be broken down into possibilities.

—AUTHOR UNKNOWN

Find ecstasy in life; the mere sense of living is joy enough.

—EMILY DICKINSON

*Do what makes you happy, be with who makes you smile,
laugh as much as you breathe, and love as long as you live.*

—RACHEL ANN NUNES

Think big thoughts but relish small pleasures.

—H. JACKSON BROWN JR.

Don't be pushed around by the fears in your mind.
Be led by the dreams in your heart.

—ROY T. BENNETT

Remember to look up at the stars and not down at your feet.
Try to make sense of what you see and wonder about
what makes the universe exist. Be curious.

—STEPHEN HAWKING

262

Enjoy the little things in life because one day you'll look back
and realize they were the big things.

—KURT VONNEGUT

Take time to look...

—GEORGIA O'KEEFE

If you're too busy to enjoy life, you're too busy.

—JEFF DAVIDSON

Thousands of things go right for you every day.

—ROB BREZSNY

Don't wait for extraordinary opportunities.
Seize common occasions and make them great.

—ORISON SWETT MARDEN

Each morning we are born again.
What we do today is what matters most.

—THE BUDDHA

Because inner peace and inner joy are independent of worldly
circumstances, they are available to you anyplace and anytime.

—CHADE-MENG TAN

It is possible to live happily ever after on a day-to-day basis.

—MARGARET WANDER BONANNO

Taking time to do nothing often brings everything
into perspective.

—DOE ZANTAMATA

Live simply. Dream big. Be grateful. Give love. Laugh lots.

—Paulo Coelho

*Wake at dawn with winged heart
and give thanks for another day of loving.*

—Kahlil Gibran

Life always offers you a second chance. It's called tomorrow.

—Nicholas Sparks

*...give to the world the best that you have,
and the best will come back to you.*

—Madeline S. Bridges

Be bold, be bold, and everywhere be bold.

—Edmund Spencer

Only I can change my life.
No one can do it for me.

—CAROL BURNETT

Above all, keep it simple.

—AUGUSTE ESCOFFIER

Do what you love and do it often.

—AUTHOR UNKNOWN

Every morning we are born again.

—THE BUDDHA

Live life as if everything is rigged in your favor.

—RUMI

Each step is the journey;
a single note the song.

—ARLENE GAY LEVINE

Author Index

268

270

271

About the Author

June Cotner is the author of thirty-six books, including the best-selling *Graces, Bedside Prayers,* and *House Blessings.* Her books altogether have sold more than one million copies and have been featured in many national publications, including *USA Today, Better Homes & Gardens, Woman's Day,* and *Family Circle.* June has appeared on national television and radio programs.

In 2011, June adopted Indy, a chocolate lab/Doberman mix (a LabraDobie!), from the Freedom Tails program at Stafford Creek Corrections Center in Aberdeen, Washington. June works with Indy daily to build on the wonderful obedience skills he mastered in the program. She and Indy have appeared on the

television shows *AM Northwest* (Portland, OR) and *New Day Northwest* (Seattle). June is also active in her local Lions Club and Poulsbo Friends of the Library.

A graduate of the University of California at Berkeley, June is the mother of two grown children and lives in Poulsbo, Washington with her husband. Her hobbies include hiking, paper crafting, and spending time with her four grandchildren.

For more information, please visit June's website at www.junecotner.com.

Mango Publishing, established in 2014, publishes an eclectic list of books by diverse authors—both new and established voices—on topics ranging from business, personal growth, women's empowerment, LGBTQ studies, health, and spirituality to history, popular culture, time management, decluttering, lifestyle, mental wellness, aging, and sustainable living. We were recently named 2019 and 2020's #1 fastest growing independent publisher by *Publishers Weekly*. Our success is driven by our main goal, which is to publish high quality books that will entertain readers as well as make a positive difference in their lives.

Our readers are our most important resource; we value your input, suggestions, and ideas. We'd love to hear from you—after all, we are publishing books for you!

Please stay in touch with us and follow us at:

Facebook: Mango Publishing
Twitter: @MangoPublishing
Instagram: @MangoPublishing
LinkedIn: Mango Publishing
Pinterest: Mango Publishing
Newsletter: mangopublishinggroup.com/newsletter

Join us on Mango's journey to reinvent publishing, one book at a time.